THIRD PROBLEMS

Decimal and metric edition

by

K. A. HESSE

LONGMAN

Contents

Note: For those teachers who wish their pupils to have some practice in imperial length and weight two pages have been included, 64 and 65.

Longman Group Ltd
London
Associated companies, branches and representatives throughout the world

First published 1965
Decimal and metric edition first published 1970
Third impression 1972

Pupils' ISBN 0 582 18078 3
Teachers' ISBN 0 582 18079 1

Made and printed by offset in Great Britain by
William Clowes & Sons, Limited, London, Beccles and Colchester

Special Words

Use your dictionary, if necessary, to find the meanings of the words in bold type in the following sums.

1. In the sum $23 \times 4 = 92$ which number is (a) the **multiplier**, (b) the **product** and (c) the **multiplicand**?
2. Write the nine **digits** and the **zero** which make up the Arabic Numerals.
3. Find the **average** of the numbers 4, 5 and 9.
4. Which three **consecutive** numbers follow 10?
5. Which of these is a rough **estimate** for the answer to 499×29? 12 000, 15 000 or 100 000?
6. What was the **remnant** when 24 metres of cloth were cut from a roll of cloth measuring $25\frac{1}{2}$ metres?
7. What **period** of time was there between 10 a.m. and noon?
8. The special **consignment** of goods left the **depot** at 9.30 a.m. and arrived at their **destination** at 2.15 p.m. How long did the journey take?
9. How many houses did the detective visit if he called at all the even numbered houses from 6 to 12, **inclusive**?
10. In the sum $4 \times a = 8$, which figure does the **symbol** "a" represent?
11. What is the difference between the **maximum** and **minimum** numbers formed from the digits 2, 4 and 6?
12. Which number is the **quotient** in one of these two sums?

    $104 \div 4 = 26 \qquad 25 \times 4 = 100$
13. State the **intervals** in metres if lamp-posts were placed 0·05 km apart along one side of a road.
14. When drawn do the diagonals of a square **intercept** or **intersect** each other?
15. Which of these, 50 m or 0·5 km, is an **approximate** answer to this sum:

    498 mm × 100

A School Party

1. There are 34 pupils in the class: (a) how many pairs will there be, and (b) how many groups of four?
2. The pupils agree to give 2p each for 5 weeks to pay expenses. (a) How much will each pupil give, and (b) what will be the total amount given?
3. One loaf supplies six children. How many loaves should be ordered to make sure there is enough bread for all pupils?
4. Each pupil is to have two cakes. How many cakes will be ordered if an extra half-dozen are added for members of staff?
5. There will be a small present on the Christmas tree for each pupil. The amount to be spent must be not more than 6p per pupil. What is the most that can be spent on presents?
6. Four bottles of orange squash have been given by a shop-keeper. If each bottle makes enough drinks for 12 pupils, how many of the pupils can have two drinks each?
7. There will be two games of musical chairs, a half of the pupils each time. If there will be two chairs less than the number taking part at the beginning of each game, how many chairs will be needed?
8. Each of 3 bench seats will take 6 pupils. How many chairs will be needed so that all can be seated, including 4 members of staff?
9. How long does a party last, if held from 5.45 p.m. to 8.15 p.m.?
10. Time for refreshments will be from 7.15 p.m. to 7.45 p.m. If six minutes are allowed for each game or dance how many should be prepared for in the programme?

Puzzles

A. Blue train leaves London to travel to Brighton at the same time as Green train leaves Brighton to travel to London. If Blue train travels at 50 m.p.h. and Green train travels at 25 m.p.h. which train will be nearer to London when they meet?

B. "A 50p coin is an equilateral heptagon."
Which word is missing?

C. John's pace is twenty-eight centimetres more than a half of its length. How long is his pace?

Dates

John Brown's date of birth is 17.9.66.

1. Write out in full his date of birth.
2. In which year will John be 16?
3. How much younger than John is his brother whose date of birth is 20th October 1968?
4. Give the date of birth of John's sister who is exactly two years and five days older than he is.
5. State John's age on 20th January 1974.
6. State John's age on 31st August 1975.

---

7. From the 3rd to the 7th May is 4 days. How long is it from
   3rd June to 15th June? 14th May to 31st May?
   20th Apr. to 6th May? 17 Nov. to 9th Dec.?
8. How many days are there altogether from 1st October to 1st November inclusive?
9. A fair opens on 30th July and closes on 8th August. For how many days is the fair held?
10. Our stay in a hotel is booked from noon 23rd August until noon 2nd September? For how many days should we be charged?
11. If an eight days' tour commences on 25th June on which date should it end?
12. If a boys' exhibition opens on 29th December 1970 for ten days on which date does it close?
13. How many days are there from 27th Jan. to 10th Feb.?
14. How many days are there from 23rd February 1972 to 5th March 1972 inclusive?
15. Veronica should have a birthday only every fourth year. Explain why this is so.
16. How many days are there from 20th February 1972 to 20th March 1972 inclusive?
17. How old will Alice be on 1st September 1980 if her date of birth is 28.2.66?

You can make any number, no matter how big, by using some or all of the digits 1, 2, 3, 4, 5, 6, 7, 8, and 9 together with a place-holder 0, which we call a **zero**. Those nine digits and the zero are known as the **arabic numerals,** and allow us to arrange our counting into groups of ten—sometimes referred to as "base ten". We can use any digit as often as we like in one number, each time having a different value according to its place.

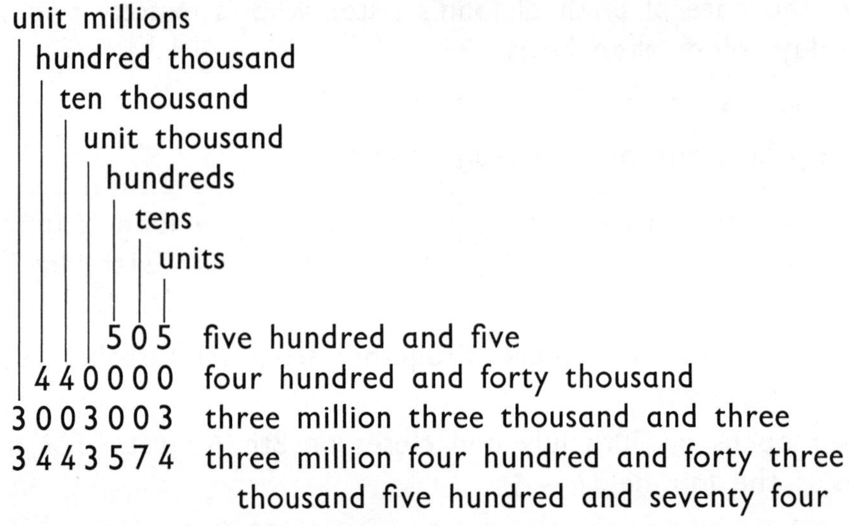

Notice that our columns are grouped in threes—units, tens and hundreds. When we come to the fourth column we call the group thousands but still describe them as we did the first three columns. To remind us that the "four hundred and forty" is not in the first three columns but in the second group of three, being the number of thousands, we have a space between the thousand place and the hundred place. In the same way we have a space between the million place and the hundred thousand place.

1. Write in figures:
   (a) six thousand seven hundred and thirty-two. (b) two thousand and eighty. (c) fifteen thousand and nineteen.
2. Write in words: 16 400; 65 062; 80 709; 10 018.

3. State the value of the figure 5 in 18 514.
4. State the value of the figure 3 in 13 060.
5. State the value of the figure 8 in 8 007 210.
6. State the value of the figure 9 in 4 392 500.

Decimals

1. In which number column does the 8 appear?
   £28 £8·50 £16·80 £0·38
   81·6 2·8 9·68 28·07
2. In which number column does the 4 appear?
   £471 £0·04 10·4 20·74
3. Multiply each of these numbers by 10:
   62 17·5 240·8 0·9 9 10·2
4. Multiply each of these numbers by 100:
   60 6 0·6 0·4 1·4 10·7 0·1
5. Divide each of these numbers by 100:
   700 170 80 3 070 2 400 3 090
6. What is the value of the figure 6 in each of these numbers?
   4·6 460 46·0 4·60 0·6
7. Write each of these numbers as a vulgar fraction:
   0·9 0·7 0·4 0·1 0·8 0·5 0·3 0·6
8. Divide each of these numbers by 100:
   5 400 54 60 6 4 3 207
9. Multiply each of these numbers by 100:
   23 0·6 2·37 0·24 0·08 1·09
10. Write each of the following numbers first as a decimal and then as a vulgar fraction:
    3 tenths 24 hundredths 18 hundredths
    7 tenths 45 hundredths 36 hundredths
    9 tenths 6 hundredths 4 hundredths
11. Complete:
    12·3 =one ten, two units and three.. ..
    4·56=four units, five.. ..and six.. ..
    3·07=three units, no tenths and seven.. ..
    7·94=.. ..
12. What is the value of the figure 3 in each of these numbers?
    1·03 10·3 307·5 20·63
13. Write each of these vulgar fractions as a decimal:
    $\frac{3}{10}$ $\frac{1}{10}$ $\frac{17}{100}$ $\frac{89}{100}$ $\frac{3}{100}$ $\frac{1}{5}$ $\frac{4}{5}$

The Nearest Quantity

Measure each of these lines to the nearest centimetre:

1. ______________________________

2. ____

3. ___________ 4. ________________________

Measure each of these lines to the nearest millimetre:

5. ___________ ________________________

6. _______________ ____________________

7. Which of these numbers is nearest to 10: 7, 13 or 11?

8. Which of these numbers is nearest to 40: 36, 42 or 39?

9. State each of these quantities to the nearest 10:
£67 32 tons $54 119 kg

10. Which of these numbers is nearest to 1 000: 909 1 009 1 090?

Write this number, 63 538 to the nearest

11. ten, hundred, thousand,

A town used on three consecutive days the following amounts of water:
790 864 kl 1 063 204 kl 908 798 kl

12. Find the total amount used and state your answer to the nearest thousand kilolitres.

A dealer bought nine pianos at an auction for £75.

13. Find the price of one piano to the nearest fifty p.

A furnisher found that in three rooms of a hotel he had laid the following lengths of carpet: 11 m 30 cm, 8 m 93 cm and 10 m 15 cm.

14. Find the total length of carpet used and state the answer to the next nearest half-metre.

Which is the nearest whole number to each of these quantities?

15. $3\frac{3}{4}$, $13\frac{7}{16}$, $1\frac{1}{2}+1\frac{3}{4}$, $5\frac{1}{4}-1\frac{1}{2}$, $12p-7\frac{1}{2}p$

A man working from 7.30 a.m. to 5 p.m., Monday to Friday, inclusive, has breakfast from 8.45 a.m. to 9 a.m. and lunch from 12.30 p.m. to 1.30 p.m.

16. Find (a) the amount of time worked each day, and (b) the total for the week to the next nearest half-hour.

17. If the man was paid at the rate of 42p per hour what did he gain by being paid to the nearest half-hour?

1. Write in figures:
   (a) Seventy thousand eight hundred.
   (b) Nineteen thousand eight hundred and forty-five.
   (c) Five hundred and sixteen thousand and ninety.
   (d) Two million.
   (e) Ten million nine hundred and eighty thousand.
   (f) Forty million nine hundred and thirteen thousand one hundred and seventy-four.
2. Multiply each of these numbers by 100:
   407; 660; 7 304; 17 800;
3. Divide each of these numbers by 100:
   700; 40 600; 708 000; 16 908 000;
4. State the value of the eight in 685 000.
5. Write a half-million in figures.
6. Write ten and a half million in figures.
7. Complete these columns showing the estimated population:

United Kingdom	Males	Females	Total
England and Wales	23 562 376	24 828 265	
Scotland	2 489 807	2 698 479	
Northern Ireland	727 097	764 084	
Total			

8. State the estimated total of the population of the United Kingdom complete to the nearest thousand.
9. If the population of the United Kingdom was 51 430 000 in 1957 and 5 5068 000 in 1967 state the increase during these 10 years.
10. In June 1967 there were 14 510 000 television licences and in June 1968 there were 15 196 000. What was the increase in the year?
11. In June 1966 there were 2 593 000 wireless licences and in June 1967 there were 2 549 000. What was the decrease in the year?

Bills

One kilogramme of apples costs 18p. Say what must be paid for:

1. 2 kg $\frac{1}{2}$ kg   500 g   1·5 kg   250 g $3\frac{1}{2}$ kg

Curtaining costs 80p per metre. Say what should be charged for:

2. 50 cm   20 cm   70 cm   2·25 m   3·5 m

One dozen eggs costs 24p. Find the cost at this price of:

3. 6 eggs   9 eggs $1\frac{1}{2}$ doz. eggs $3\frac{1}{4}$ doz. eggs

A man is paid 44p per hour. At this rate find what he should be paid to work:

4. 2 hours, $3\frac{1}{2}$ hr,   from 8.45 a.m. to 2.15 p.m.
5. From 7.30 a.m. to 5 p.m., having a one-hour stop for lunch.
6. For three days from 8 a.m. to 6 p.m. each day, having a one and a quarter hour stop for lunch.

Oil is 18p per litre, 75p per 5-litres or £2·78 per 20-litre drum.

7. What is the price per litre at the 5-litre rate?
8. What is the price per 5-litres at the litre rate?
9. What is saved by buying 5-litres at the 5-litre rate instead of the litre rate?
10. What is saved by buying a 20-litre drum instead of 20 litres at the 5-litre rate?

One ton of coal costs £13·90. Fifty kilogrammes of the same coal cost 76p.

11. What should be paid for $1\frac{1}{2}$ tons of coal?
12. What is the cost of 50 kilogrammes of coal at the ton rate?
13. What is saved by buying one ton of coal at the ton rate rather than one ton at the fifty-kilogramme rate?

Find the total cost of the following bills:

14. 5 kg of potatoes @ 1 kg for $3\frac{1}{2}$p; $\frac{1}{2}$ kg of carrots @ 9p per kg; 750 g of tomatoes @ 28p per kg; 15 eggs @ 30p per dozen.
15. 1 ton 250 kg of coal @ £14·20 per ton; 350 kg of coke @ 79p per 50 kg; 2 sacks of wood @ 35p each.

1. What portion of this figure is shaded?
2. What portion of this figure are two of the shaded squares?

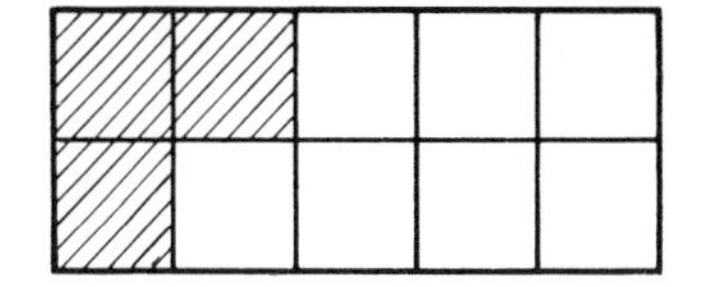

3. What is the length of this line? ————————————————
4. What length is (a) one-half of it, and (b) one-third of it?
5. What part of one week are two days?
6. What is $\frac{2}{3}$ of the contents of a milk churn holding 34·5 l?
7. What should be the weight of a half of the contents of a half kilogramme packet of rice?
8. Decrease ten thousand by one-fifth.
9. Increase a half-million by one-tenth.
10. Find the cost of a quarter gross of pencils at £2·58 per gross.
11. What should be paid for 18 eggs at 29p per dozen?
12. A farmer has a flock of 175 sheep. How many must he sell in order to decrease the size of his flock by one-fifth?
13. What sum of money equals two-fifths of one hundred pounds?
14. What part of thirty tons are five tons?
15. When Mary had read 25 pages of a book she found that she had read one-fifth of it. How many pages were in that book?
16. If $\frac{2}{3}$ of 12 is 8 what part of 24 is 16?
17. If 10 is $\frac{2}{5}$ of 25 what part of 25 is 15?
18. If 14 is $\frac{1}{4}$ of 56 (a) what part of 56 is 7, and
(b) what part of 56 is 21?
19. What part of one hour is twenty-four minutes?
20. State how much £$\frac{5}{4}$ is in decimals.
21. What is the total amount of potatoes collected from a farm if a lorry fetches $2\frac{3}{4}$ tons one day, $2\frac{1}{2}$ tons the next day and $3\frac{1}{4}$ tons the next?
22. How many 5 ml doses are there in a $\frac{1}{2}$ litre bottle of medicine?
23. What is the total working time if a man commences work at 7.30 a.m. and stops at 5 p.m., but is allowed $\frac{1}{4}$ hr during the morning and $\frac{1}{4}$ hr during the afternoon for tea breaks and $1\frac{1}{4}$ hr for lunch?

Where possible select the correct answer from inside the brackets.

1. Multiplication is to product as subtraction is to (remainder, total, difference, quotient).
2. A Leap Year has (364, 365, 356, 366) days.
3. Minus is the opposite of (divide, subtract, plus, multiply).
4. 0·75 of £1 is (more, same, less) value than 75p.
5. A gross is (100, 112, 144, 150).
6. One day consists of (12 hours, 24 hours, 36 hours, 48 hours).
7. p.m. is (at, before, after, instead of) noon.
8. $\frac{3}{8}$ is smaller than ($\frac{3}{16}$, $\frac{1}{4}$, $\frac{3}{4}$) but larger than ($\frac{3}{4}$, $\frac{3}{5}$, $\frac{3}{7}$, $\frac{3}{11}$).
9. To increase speed means that the journey will be (shorter, longer, quicker).
10. For a journey to take less time the speed must be (increased, decreased).
11. If $\frac{1}{4}$ of a number is 8 that number must be (2, 4, 12, 16, 32).
12. If twice a number is 10 that number must be (20, 15, 5, 2).
13. If 4 is $\frac{1}{3}$ of a number $\frac{1}{6}$ of that number must be (2, 8, 12, 24).
14. If $\frac{1}{10}$ of 1 kg=100 g then $\frac{1}{10}$ of 1 litre=(10, 100, 1 000) ml.
15. The product of 4 and 12 is (3, 8, 16, 48).
16. The difference between 20 and 5 is (4, 15, 25, 100).
17. A square is always (an oblong, a rectangle).
18. A rectangle is (always, either, never) an oblong or a square.
19. A triangle (sometimes, never, always) has three sides.
20. If 1 cc of water weighs one gramme and 1 ml of water equals 1 cc of water, then 1 litre of water weighs (100, 1 000, 10 000) grammes.
21. If Molly is younger than Mary and Mary is younger than Maisy, then (Molly, Mary, Maisy) is the oldest.
22. Which is the smallest of three numbers if the first is larger than the second number, and the first number is smaller than the third?
23. Which is the larger (half a dozen dozen loaves or six dozen dozen loaves)?
24. Is a fifty kilogramme sack of coal (heavier than, lighter than or the same as) a fifty kilogramme sack of coke?

1. Write in words: 206 040.

2. Find the difference between one million thirteen thousand nine-hundred, and one million seventy-three thousand and ninety.

3. $2{\cdot}06 \div 100 =$ $\quad$ $0{\cdot}032 \times 10 =$ $\quad$ $£1{\cdot}05 \div 10 =$

4. Change £0·70 to pence $\quad$ and $9\frac{1}{2}$p to pounds

5. Write one pound seven pence in figures.

6. 6 fives plus 2 fifties minus seven tens plus ten twos.

Complete:

7.	1·37 l = l ml	0·708 kl = l	2 kl 60 l = kl
8.	3·80 cm = cm mm	0·09 km = m	3 m 5 cm = m
9.	95 min. = hr min.	$\frac{3}{4}$ min. = sec.	$\frac{2}{5}$ hr = min.
10.	64 hr = days hr	3 wk = days	$1\frac{1}{2}$ yr = mth
11.	3·3 g = g mg.	0·25 ton = kg	1 kg 9 g = kg

12. 8.20 a.m. to 10.10 a.m. = hr. min.

13. 10.50 p.m. to 2.45 a.m. = hr min.

14. 27th August to 5th October = days

15. 16th December 1971 to 20th January 1972 = days

16. 21st February 1972 to 30th March 1972 = days

Work the following:

17. $£93{\cdot}65 + £8{\cdot}70 + 86\frac{1}{2}\text{p} + 40\frac{1}{2}\text{p}$ $\quad$ $£20{\cdot}30 - £1{\cdot}08\frac{1}{2}$

18. Deduct ninety and a half pence from three pounds seven.

19. $£2{\cdot}70\frac{1}{2} \times 9$ $\quad$ $£10{\cdot}40 \div 11$

20. 750 g of haddock at $37\frac{1}{2}$p per kilogramme.

21. $10\frac{1}{2}$ litres of milk at 9p per litre.

22. 7 hr 35 min. − 2 hr 47 min.
    6 days 3 hr − 4 days 15 hr

23. 2 min. 52 sec. × 9 $\quad$ 42 hr 24 min. ÷ 12

24. 20·8 mm + 7·6 mm + 1·75 cm + 0·8 cm

25. 1·03 kg − 230·5 g $\quad$ 209·5 m × 12

26. 2·068 tons ÷ 8 $\quad$ 0·96 kl ÷ 11

By Express Bus

A SOUTH COAST EXPRESS BUS SERVICE					
Brighton dep.	08·25	14.35	Portsmouth dep.	08.45	15.50
Worthing ,,	09.28	15.36	Bognor Regis ,,	09.52	16.59
Bognor Regis ,,	10.00	16.12	Worthing ,,	10.38	17.46
Portsmouth arr.	11.10	17.24	Brighton arr.	11.32	18.42

1. When does the first bus from Brighton arrive at Bognor Regis?
2. When is the second bus from Portsmouth due at Bognor Regis?
3. How long does the afternoon bus from Brighton take to travel to Worthing?
4. How long does the morning bus take to travel from Portsmouth to Worthing?
5. At what time does the 14.35 bus from Brighton arrive at Portsmouth?
6. How long does the morning journey take from Brighton to Portsmouth?
7. Which of the two buses from Brighton to Portsmouth takes the least travelling time?
8. Which is the faster service from Portsmouth to Brighton, morning or afternoon?
9. If you travelled by the first bus from Brighton to Portsmouth at what time could you get the next bus back to Brighton?
10. If you travelled from Portsmouth in the morning how long could you stay in Brighton in order to return the same day?
11. How long would be the quickest return journey you could make from Brighton to Worthing?
12. What is the longest stay you could make in Worthing during one day if you lived in Brighton?
13. What is the longest stay you could make during one day in Worthing if you lived in Portsmouth?

A milkman commences his duties at 7 a.m. and ends them at 2 p.m. He sets out on his round at 7.20 a.m. and returns at 12.35 p.m.

1. How long is the milkman's working day?
2. How long is he in delivering the milk bottles?
3. How long is he occupied in duties at the dairy?
4. On Saturdays collecting money as well as delivering the milk takes an extra $2\frac{1}{4}$ hours. At what time would you expect him to finish (a) delivery, (b) his duties?
5. Work out the total number of hours worked in a normal week of six working days, including Saturday.

The first load of milk consists of 40 crates, each holding 20 cartons. Later a lorry arrives with 15 full crates and takes away those with empty cartons. A carton holds 600 ml of milk.

6. What is the total consignment of cartons to be delivered?
7. What is the total amount in litres?
8. How many cartons are delivered on a day when the milkman returns to the dairy with $2\frac{1}{2}$ crates of cartons undelivered?
9. At 9p per litre what is the value of the first consgnment?
10. What is the total value of milk delivered on the day when $4\frac{1}{2}$ crates of full cartons are returned?
11. What is the weekly payment from a family which takes 3 cartons each day except Sunday, when 4 cartons are needed?
12. If the complete milk round extends for $6\frac{1}{2}$ kilometres, what is the total distance covered for that truck in one week?

Of 405 pupils present in a day school 37 did not take milk. $12\frac{1}{3}$ crates of pupils' milk were ordered, each crate holding 6 rows with 5 cartons per row. Each carton holds 200 ml of milk.

13. How many cartons of milk were ordered?
14. How many pupils would have two cartons each to use up the extra cartons?
15. If the same quantity were delivered each day what was the total quantity in litres for one week?
16. Find the value of the week's supply at 9p per litre

The Coalman

On the coalman's lorry were 75 full bags, awaiting delivery in lots of five to each house. Each bag contained fifty kilogrammes of coal.

1. How many houses was the coalman to visit?
2. He charged a lady £3·90 for five bags. What was the price per 50 kilogrammes?
3. What change did the lady receive for a five-pound note?
4. What was the price per metric ton?
5. What was the total weight of coal on the lorry in tons?
6. How many 50 kilogrammes equal one ton?

The coal merchant was told that there were two trucks at the railway sidings containing 12 tons 950 kg and 12 tons 850 kg of coal awaiting collection. A lorry was sent to collect the coal, which was to be weighed into fifty kilogramme bags ready for delivery and made up into 6 equal loads.

7. Find the total amount of coal in the two trucks.
8. How many bags were to be on the lorry at each load?
9. After 4 journeys the lorry broke down. How much coal should there have been still at the railway sidings?

Another lorry was then sent to a nearby colliery to collect some coal. There the lorry was weighed, then filled with coal and weighed again. The first weight was 2 tons 600 kg and the second was 7 tons 450 kg.

10. How much coal was there on the lorry?
11. If the lorry made eight similar visits altogether to the colliery, what would be the total amount of coal collected?
12. How much coal would be needed to deliver 175 fifty kilogramme bags?

1. If one-half of a number is 77 what is the number?
2. 320 trees are to be felled. How many are left standing when one-quarter of them have been cut?
3. When a warship arrived in port three-quarters of the crew were allowed to go on leave. If there was a crew of 900 how many would be left on board?
4. What part of a twelve metre wall is a two-metre section?
5. In order to erect a 300 cm gate-post one-quarter of it had to be buried. (a) How deep was the hole, and (b) how high was the post above ground?
6. What part of 20 equals $\frac{1}{6}$ of 30?
7. What part of one metre is $\frac{1}{6}$ of three metres?
8. What part of four tons is ten fifty kilogrammes?
9. If a car travelled for 13 km in $\frac{1}{4}$ hour, how far should it have travelled in one hour if it continued at the same speed?
10. $3\frac{1}{2}$ cm were cut from a fifteen centimetre steel rod. What length of the rod remained?
11. If gold braid costs 3p for 5 cm what should be the charge for $1\frac{1}{2}$ metres of it?
12. Don decided to save $\frac{1}{3}$ of his pocket money. How much should he save to the nearest penny when it is (a) 50p and (b) 65p?

13. If $\frac{1}{3}$ of a sum of money was £15·50 what was the sum?
14. A tar machine re-surfaces $\frac{1}{2}$ kilometre of road in one day. What length of road will be re-surfaced at this rate in 25 days?
15. It was found that 10 tons of iron ore produced one ton of good iron. How much good iron should be produced from a half-million tons of the same ore?
16. A football ground holds 42 000 people. $\frac{1}{6}$ of the places are reserved at 45p each, $\frac{1}{3}$ of them are reserved at 25p each and the rest are unreserved at 20p each. (a) How many places are there at the dearest price, and (b) how many are there at the cheapest price?

Travelling by Bus

Here is a time-table showing the principal stops made on a daily bus service between Coventry and Manchester.

COVENTRY–BIRMINGHAM–MANCHESTER				
Weekdays and Sundays				
Coventry	dep.	07.50	10.27	16.10
Birmingham	arr.	08.48	11.13	16.52
	dep.	09.00	11.18	17.00
Wolverhampton	dep.	09.48	12.06	17.44
Newcastle-u-Lyme	arr.	11.10	13.28	19.05
	dep.	11.18	14.30	20.10
Manchester	arr.	13.10	16.46	22.05

1. If I wished to be in Manchester by 16.00 at what time should I catch a bus at Coventry?
2. If I wished to be in Wolverhampton by 13.00 at what time should I catch a bus at Birmingham?
3. State how long the first service stops at Birmingham.
4. Which of the three buses stops longest at Birmingham?
5. Which bus stops longest at Newcastle-under-Lyme?
6. Which bus travels fastest between Coventry and Birmingham?
7. Which is the slowest travelling bus between Newcastle-under-Lyme and Manchester?
8. What is the latest time you could leave Birmingham in order to keep an appointment at 14.00 at Newcastle-under-Lyme?
9. If you allow thirty-five minutes to travel from home to the bus station at Birmingham what is the latest time you can leave home to catch a bus that will get you to Newcastle-under-Lyme by 14.00?
10. On the Fridays before a bank holiday an extra bus leaves Coventry at 19.50 and keeps the same schedule as that which leaves at 07.50. At what time would you expect to arrive at Manchester on this extra bus?

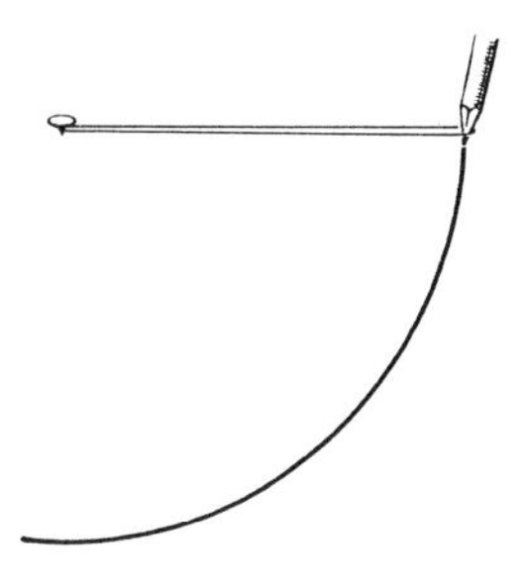

Drawing large circles cannot be done with a pair of ordinary compasses. An easy and cheap way is to fix a drawing-pin or something suitable at the centre of the circle to hold a loop of cotton or string. In the other end of the loop is firmly held a pencil or piece of chalk which marks out the circle. By this means you can draw quite large circles on the playground, on the playing field, on a wall, etc.

1. What special name do we give to the line made by the pencil or chalk?
2. What special name do we give to the distance from this line to the centre of the circle?
3. What special name do we give to the line which divides a circle into halves?

Try to imagine the hour hand of a clock remaining at 12 as the minute hand continues to turn. The amount by which the two hands become separated can be measured in **degrees**. A degree is found by dividing the circumference of a circle into 360 equal parts and making marks. If any two of those marks next to each other on the circumference are joined to the centre, the space between them is one degree.

4. Make a right angle by folding a circle twice. Work out how many degrees there are in a right angle.
5. If the hour hand is at 12 and the minute hand points to 3 how many degrees are there between them?
6. Through how many degrees does the minute hand move from 12 to 6?
7. Through how many degrees does the minute hand move from 12 to 9?
8. Through how many right-angles does a line turn when making a complete circle?
9. Through how many degrees has the minute hand turned in moving from 3 o'clock to 9 o'clock?

C

A B

1. Draw a line 6 centimetres long. Mark it AB. Set your compasses at 8 centimetres and, with the point on A, make an arc above the line as in the diagram.
2. Repeat this at B with a radius of 10 cm so that the two arcs intersect at C. Join C to A and to B.
3. Write the length of each side on your drawing.
4. Measure the angle CAB.
5. If possible obtain a piece of string over 2 metres long. Tie a knot about 5 cm from the end. From that knot measure 3 times 15 cm and tie another knot, and another 4 times 15 cm from that, and still another 5 times 15 cm from that knot. Now tie the ends of the string together so that the first and last knots come together.
6. Stretch out your string on the ground so that the portions between the knots are straight, thus forming a triangle. Measure the angles and compare them with those in your drawing.

---

7. On a separate sheet of paper draw a circle having a radius of 10 cm. Mark the centre M.

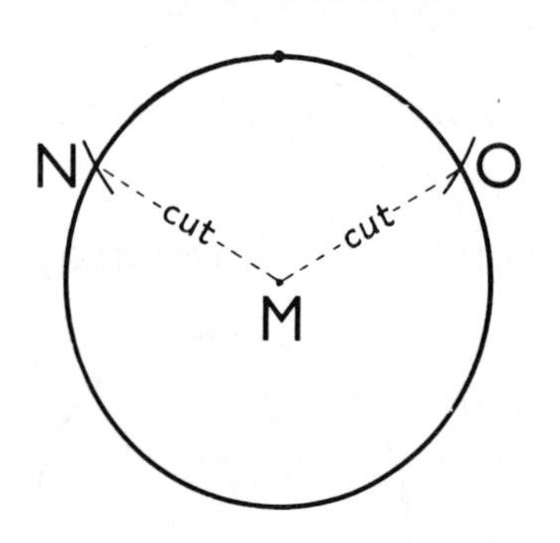

8. Place the point of the compasses on the circumference of the circle and mark it on either side as in the diagram. Join M to N and M to O.
9. Cut out your circle and also cut from it the portion NMO.

0. Bring together the straight edges of the remaining portion and fix.

11. What is the shape formed by the sector of your circle?
12. What would be the shape of the new surface if your cone was cut across horizontally?
13. What would be the shape of the new surface if your cone was cut in a slanting direction without reaching the base?

Perimeters

1. What is the length of this oblong?
2. What is its width?
3. Find the distance all round it. (This is the perimeter.)
4. Draw a rectangle 8·5 cm long and 5 cm wide.
5. What is the perimeter of your rectangle?
6. Draw a square with sides five centimetres long and say what is its perimeter.
7. What is the perimeter of a square having sides of 8 cm?
8. What would be the length of the sides of a square which had a perimeter of 4 centimetres?
9. What would be the length of the sides of a square which had a perimeter of 16 centimetres?
10. Find the perimeter of a square having sides of 7·5 cm
11. Find the perimeter of an oblong having sides of 12 cm 4 mm and 8·6 centimetres.
12. Use a piece of cotton, wool, or string to find the perimeter of (a) the circle, and (b) the curved shape.

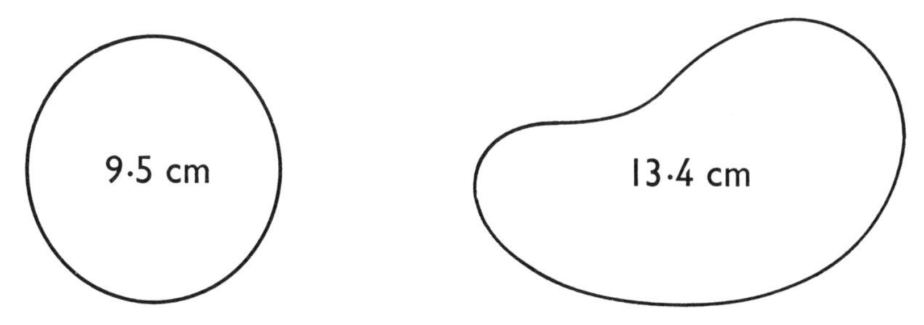

13. Use a piece of string to find the measurements of your wrist, ankle, waist and chest.
14. Estimate some distances and perimeters of shapes in the playground, or on the playing field, and then check them with a trundle wheel, measuring tape, metre stick or some suitable measuring device.

Perimeters

1. Find the perimeter of the oblong.
2. Find the perimeter of the parallelogram.
3. Think how they are alike and how they are different.

Parallelogram

Find the perimeter of an oblong 16 cm long and 13 cm wide.

Find the perimeter of a parallelogram having long sides of 11 cm and short sides of $7\frac{1}{2}$ cm.

Rhombus

6. Find the perimeter of this rhombus.
7. Find the perimeter of this square.
8. Think

(a) how a square is different from a rhombus;
(b) how a square is like a rhombus;
(c) how a square is like an oblong;
(d) how a square is different from an oblong;
(e) how a rhombus is the same as a parallelogram;
(f) how a parallelogram is different from a rhombus.

Square

9. What is the perimeter of a rectangular field which is 108 metres long and 76 metres wide?
10. Find the perimeter of a square plot having sides of 50 m.
11. Find the size of a square having a perimeter of 40 m.
12. Find the perimeter of a rectangular sheet of plywood which is 122 cm 4 mm long and 84 cm wide.
13. Find the perimeter of a rectangular plot $\frac{1}{2}$ km by $\frac{1}{4}$ km.
14. Find the cost of fencing a square plot on 3 sides, each 167 m long, at a cost of £2 per metre.
15. Find the perimeter of a rectangular building plot 98 m long and 10 m 65 cm wide.

Unequal Sharing (1)

Mother has the same number of bottles of milk each weekday, but has two extra bottles on a Sunday. During the week she has 23 bottles altogether.

1. If mother did not have any extra on Sunday what would be the total number of bottles for the week?
2. How many would that be for each day?
3. How many bottles of milk did mother have on a Sunday?

Tom is older than Ann, who has less pocket money. They decided to buy mother a birthday present for $62\frac{1}{2}$p, and Tom agreed to pay $12\frac{1}{2}$p more than Ann.

4. After Tom had put out his $12\frac{1}{2}$p how much was left to be paid by both of them together?
5. How much of that did each pay?
6. How much was paid by Ann? By Tom?
7. If Tom had agreed to pay $17\frac{1}{2}$p more than Ann how much would he have paid altogether?

In a class of 36 pupils there are four more boys than girls.

8. How many are there in the class when all the girls are present and there are as many boys as girls?
9. How many girls are there in the class?
10. How many boys are there in the class?

Dave took Dick and Harry into the woods to show them where to gather horse-chestnuts. Altogether they collected 86 conkers. Dick and Harry agreed that Dave should have 5 extra and the rest should be shared equally.

11. How many were to be shared equally?
12. Whose share was 27 conkers?
13. Whose share was 32 conkers?

A board which was 405 cm long, had to be cut into three pieces so that two were of equal length and the other was 45 cm longer.

14. How long was each of the short boards?
15. What was the length of the longest board?

Unequal Sharing (2)

1. Divide 173 to make two numbers so that one is 5 greater than the other.
2. The sum of two numbers is 208. If one is 12 greater than the other what are the two numbers?
3. The difference between two numbers is 21. Their sum is 375. What are the two numbers?
4. Two men agree to share the cost of buying a motor-car for £675. If Mr. A agrees to pay £45 more than Mr. B how much does each pay?
5. In a school of 431 pupils there are 17 more girls than boys. How many girls are there?
6. A passenger noticed that it took a plane 43 minutes longer to fly from London Airport to New York than it did on the return trip. The total flying time for the round journey was 12 hr 9 min. How long was the journey by plane from New York to London?
7. When measured soon after birth the total weight of twin babies was 6 kg 810 g. If the girl was 170 g heavier than the boy what was the weight of each?
8. It was estimated that in June 1967 there were 1 512 000 more females than males in the United Kingdom. If the total population at that time was 55 068 000 how many males and how many females were there?
9. A man travelled by jet plane to New York from London and by a propeller plane back to London. His total bill was £343·50. What was the jet fare if it was £13·70 more than the other?
10. A plot of land has to be marked out as a rectangle which has a perimeter of 240 metres, having the long sides 20 metres longer than the short sides. Find the sizes of the plot.
11. Share £510 among four men so that one receives £20 more than each of his companions.
12. The driver of an oil tanker had to deliver 6 750 litres of fuel oil to three schools, so that one had 1 350 litres more than each of the other two. How many gallons of fuel oil were in the largest consignment?

Write answers only:

1. How many oranges will be needed to give a half-orange each to 13 people?
2. On what date is the third Tuesday in June if the first Tuesday is 2nd June?
3. What is 107×25 to the nearest 100?
4. Write in figures: two million sixty thousand five hundred.
5. What sum of money is three-quarters of one hundred pounds?
6. How many people could receive 250 kg of coke each from 2 tons?
7. How much milk does mother take in 6 days at $1\frac{1}{2}$ litres per day?
8. What length of wire would be needed to form a square, having each of its sides $5\frac{1}{2}$ metres long?
9. If each pupil is to receive 200 ml of milk each morning how many litres of milk must be ordered each day for 32 pupils?

Work in your book:

10. How much is left from a plank of wood 5·5 metres long if a length of 286 cm is cut from it?
11. 380 cups and saucers have to be packed in cartons which hold 12 sets each. How many cartons will be needed?
12. What is the cost to begin keeping 2 rabbits if they cost $87\frac{1}{2}$p each and the hutch costs £1·$62\frac{1}{2}$?
13. How many 50 kilogramme sacks of coal are on a lorry which when empty weighed 1 ton 900 kg and with the sacks 4 tons 350 kg?
14. What is the difference between $\frac{1}{4}$ of 216 and $\frac{1}{3}$ of 162?
15. A square has a perimeter of 292 metres. How long is the side?
16. Draw a line AB 8·4 cm long. Draw a perpendicular CD, 5·6 cm long, from C, the centre of AB. Join D to B. How long is DB?
17. How many pupils went on a school journey if each paid 15p and the total was £8·40?
18. What would be the total cost for the month of July if your mother took $1\frac{1}{2}$ litres of milk daily at 8p per litre?

Scale Measurement

Measure these lines and complete the answers below each.

1. ____

   length=..   .. cm ..   .. mm or ..   .. cm

2. ____

   length=..   .. cm ..   .. mm or ..   .. cm

3. ________________________________

   If 1 mm represents 1 cm what length does this line represent?

4. ___________________________

   If 5 mm=20 cm what length does this line represent?

5. ____

   If 1 cm=45 m what length does this line represent?

Here is the plan of a room: scale 1 cm=50 cm (or, scale 1 mm=..   ..cm)

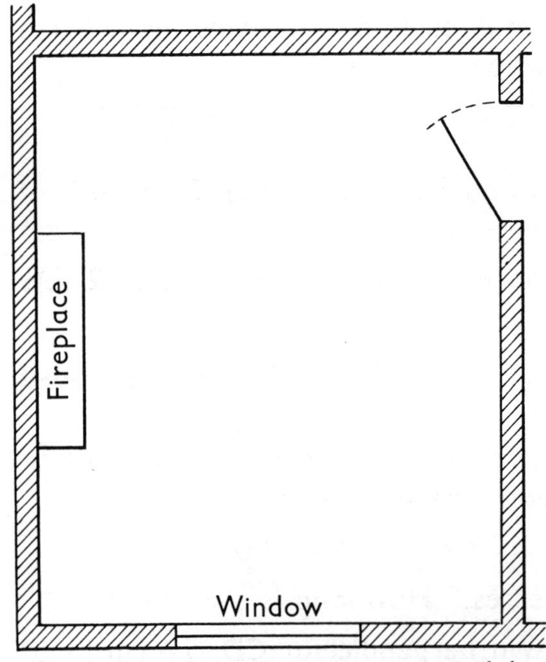

6. State the actual measurements for the following:
   (a) width of the room;
   (b) length of the room;
   (c) width of the doorway;
   (d) distance of the doorway from the nearest wall;
   (e) width of the window;
   (f) width of the fireplace.
7. Is the window fixed centrally in that wall?
8. Is the fireplace fixed centrally in that wall?
9. What length is represented by this line when drawn to the following scales:

   ____

   (a) 1 mm=1 m
   (b) 2 mm=50 cm
   (c) 2 mm=35 m
   (d) 5 mm=100 m
   (e) 5 mm=1 km
   (f) 1 cm=3 km

1. Copy this scale and add other divisions to show all the five litre intervals along the scale.

   0 25 50

2. Copy the scale below and add the necessary amounts to each of the major divisions marked on it.

   g 500 0 4 Kg

3. What length on that scale represents $2\frac{1}{2}$ kg? 3·8 kg

4. Copy the scale below and add the necessary figures to complete it.

   min. 60 0 hr.

5. What length on the above scale represents $\frac{1}{2}$ hr? $4\frac{1}{4}$ hr?

6. Here is a scale representing a petrol gauge E ¼ ½ ¾ F

When F represents	50 l	40 l	60 l	75 l
What is represented by	$\frac{1}{2}$	$\frac{1}{4}$	$\frac{3}{4}$	$\frac{3}{4}$

7. Copy the scale below and complete it.

   m 1000 0 10 Km

8. What distance is represented on that scale by

   6 cm? 12 mm? 8·7 cm? 13·5 cm?

Study the scales on a map of the British Isles. State the approximate distance in kilometres, as the crow flies, from

9. Birmingham to Leicester, Carlisle to Edinburgh.

Here is a sketch of a parcel of land showing measurements in metres.

10. Say what lengths would represent the following sides on a scale 1 cm=4 m:
    (a) the shortest side;
    (b) the opposite side.

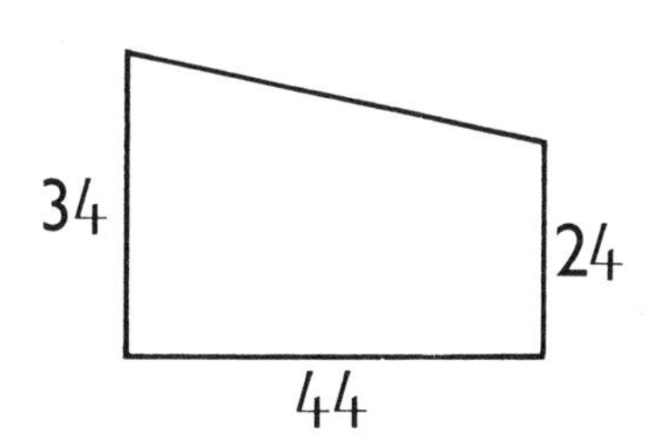

11. Make a drawing of the land drawn to a scale 1 cm=5 m.

12. Make a scale drawing of the plan of your class-room to show the position of windows, doors and your desk. Use a scale 2 cm=1 m.

When John stated that he did not have much time to play, his father said, "Well, let us see what you do with your time. There are 24 hours in one day, but that includes the hours of darkness as well as the hours of daylight."

"Yes," replied John, "but I don't count sleeping time."

"That is very important," said Father. "We must include the time you sleep as well as the time you play. Without plenty of sleep you would not enjoy your play."

A list was made like the one below showing just what John did at various times throughout one day.

Dress and undress (dress, wash, clean teeth, etc.)		7.30 a.m.	– 8 a.m.
		8.15 p.m.	– 8.30 p.m.
Meals	breakfast	8 a.m.	– 8.15 a.m.
	dinner	12.30 p.m.	– 1 p.m.
	tea	4.30 p.m.	– 5 p.m.
	supper	8 p.m.	– 8.15 p.m.
School	morning	9 a.m.	– 12 noon
	afternoon	1.30 p.m.	– 4 p.m.
Play	morning	8.15 a.m.	– 9 a.m.
	before dinner	12 noon	– 12.30 p.m.
	after dinner	1 p.m.	– 1.30 p.m.
	after school	4 p.m.	– 4.30 p.m.
	after tea	6 p.m.	– 8 p.m.
Watching television		5 p.m.	– 6 p.m.
Bed		8.30 p.m.	– 7.30 a.m.

When Father asked about odd jobs John said that some went with meal times and the rest was fun and counted with play.

Work out the times in hours, half-hours or quarter hours, copy down the six headings and put the total against each.

24 Hours with John

When John had worked out his times and found the totals, his father suggested a way by which John could show at a glance how his time was spent. It was done in this way.

Father gave John some squared paper and told him to cut strips so that each 4 squares of its length represented one hour. They were then pasted into his scrap book and looked like the diagram below.

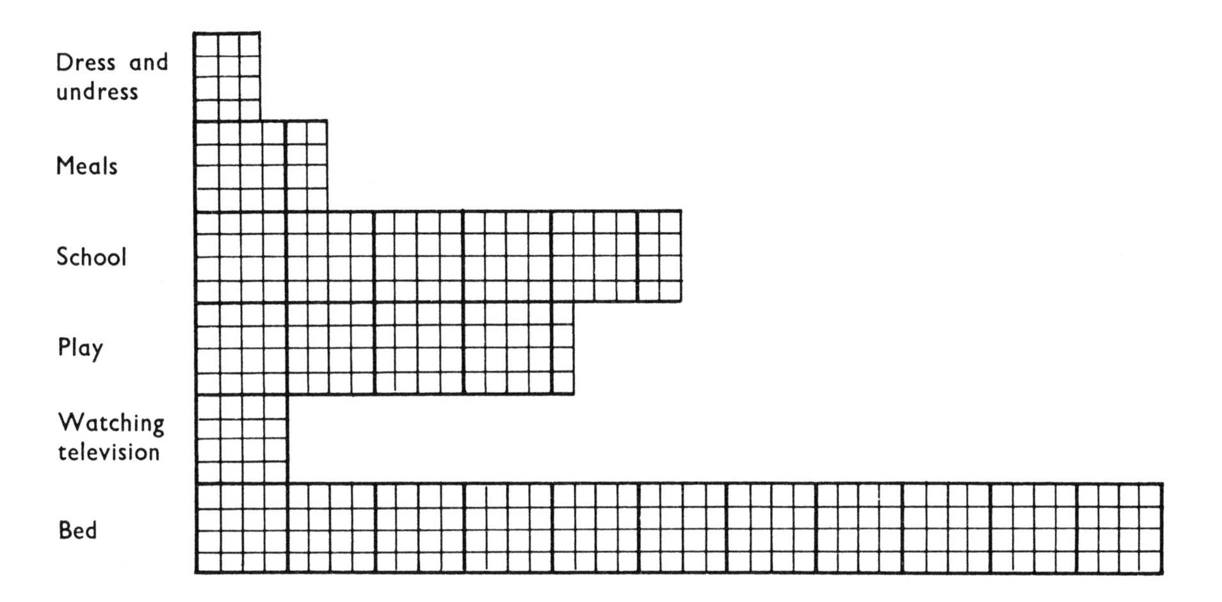

1. Four squares represent one hour. What do two squares represent?
2. What does one square stand for?
3. How did John represent $\frac{3}{4}$ hour?
4. Measure the strips and see if the lengths of them represent the same numbers of hours as you had on your list of total times.
5. Of the ways in which John spends his day what takes most time?
6. At what does John spend the least time?
7. How many hours did John spend at play on this day?
8. How much longer does he spend in school than at play?

Your Histogram

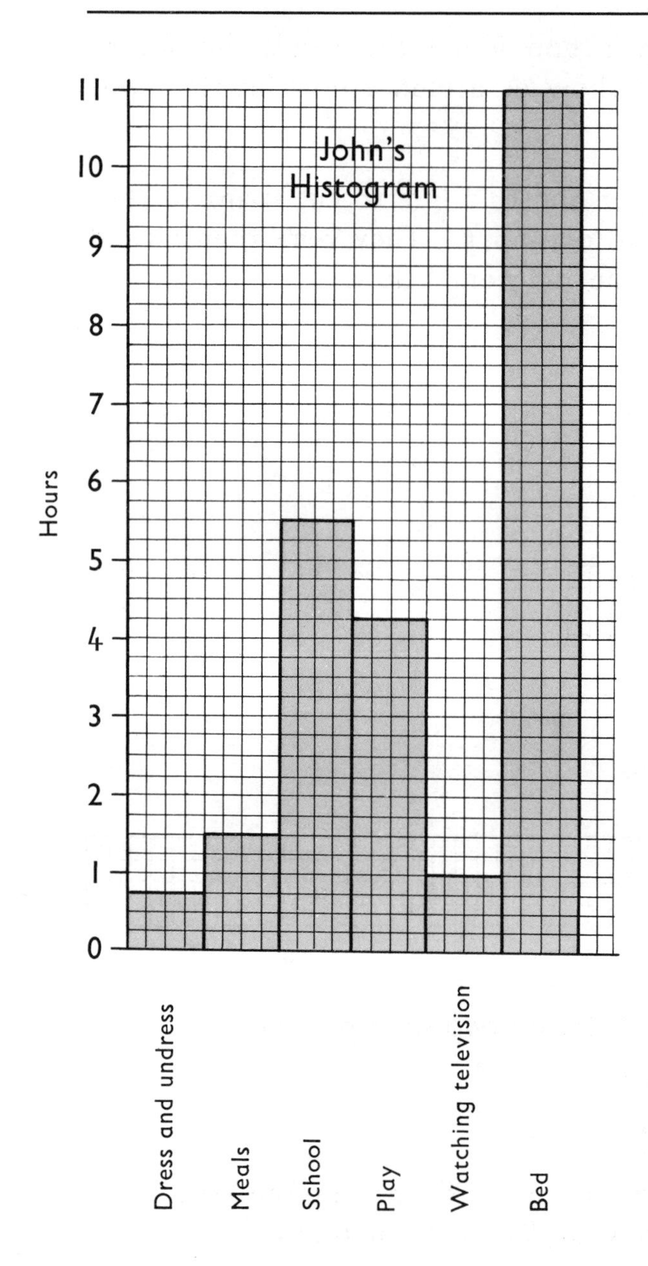

Instead of cutting strips John could have drawn a line down the side of the sheet of squared paper and marked it off in hours, starting at the bottom, counting up 4 squares and making a mark to show one hour, counting up 4 more squares for another hour and writing 2 against it, continuing in this way up the line making a mark at every fourth square—see opposite. Then he could have drawn a line along the bottom and put a mark at every fourth square for each item for the day. These marks stand for the columns instead of the strips of paper.

For the first item, "Dress and undress", he would have counted three squares up for the $\frac{3}{4}$ hour, putting a line across four squares to mark the top ready to draw in that column. When all the columns were marked and drawn in, he would have made a histogram, like the one drawn here.

1. Work out the times you spend for one day doing the things that John did. On a sheet of squared paper make a histogram to show them.

2. At what do you spend the largest part of your day?

3. At what do you spend the smallest part of your day?

4. Which activity occupies most of your day when awake?

Birthdays

Here is a histogram showing how many of the boys and girls in one class of a school had birthdays during each month of the year.

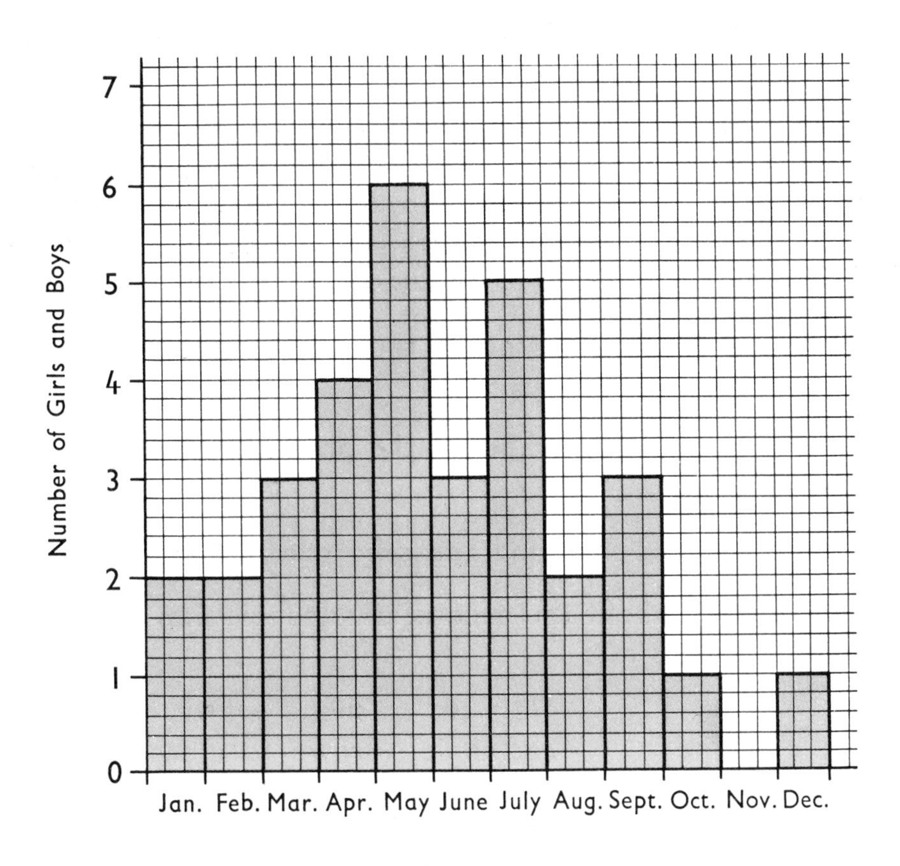

1. How many had birthdays in January?
2. How many had birthdays in April?
3. In which month was there no birthday?
4. Which month had the largest number of birthdays?
5. Which month had the next highest number of birthdays?
6. Find out from your classmates in which months are their birthdays, include your own, and make a histogram like the one above for your class.

Area

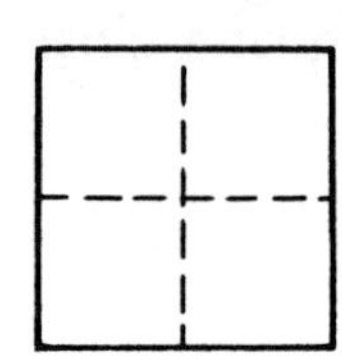

1. Measure the lengths of the sides of this square.
   So far our measurements have been of length. This square gives us a new measurement that of area, or the amount of surface. We say that a 2 cm square encloses 4 square centimetres.

Sometimes we need to measure the amount of surface enclosed or covered when a shape is not rectangular. This can be done by copying the shape on squared paper or drawing squares over it. We count the number of whole squares in the shape plus those that have $\frac{1}{2}$ or more covered.

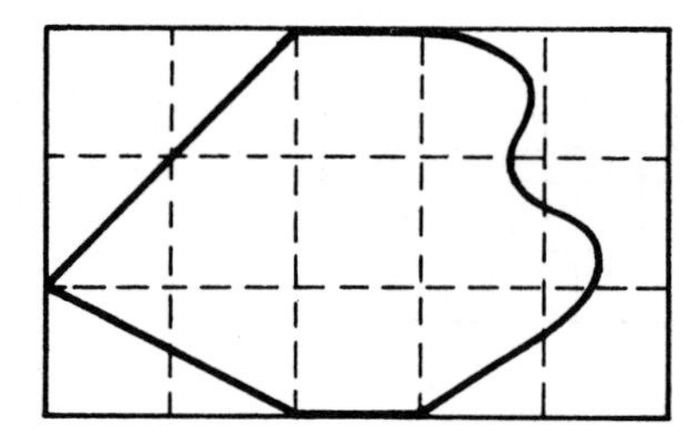

2. What is the area of the large rectangle?

3. What is the area of the irregular shape in it?

4. Find the area covered by a hand.

5. What can you say about the area of a rectangle 6 m by 4 m and that of a rectangle 8 m by 3 m?

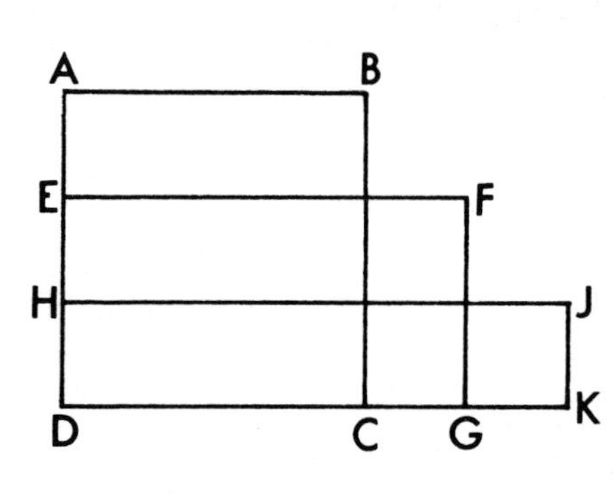

6. Here is a shape which contains several rectangles, drawn to a scale of 1 cm=4 m. Use this information to find out more about each of the rectangles below and complete the columns.

	ABCD	EFGD	HJKD
Length	12 m		
Width		8 m	
Perimeter			
Area			

7. Complete: If a square has the same.. ..as an oblong then the.. ..of the square is greater than that of the oblong.

8. Complete: In two rectangles, one 6 cm by 2 cm and the other 4 cm by 3 cm, the.. ..are equal but the.. .. are unequal.

1. Find the area of a rectangle 6 cm by 4 cm.
2. If a rectangular lawn has an area of 24 square metres and is 6 metres long, how wide is it?
3. If a rectangular carpet has an area of fifteen square metres and is three metres wide, how long is it?
4. How many square centimetres equal one square metre?
5. If a rectangular carpet has an area of twelve square metres and is three metres wide, how long is it?
6. How many square metres in a rug that is 120 cm wide and 2 m long?

7. What should it cost to make a lawn 12 m long and 10 m 30 cm wide with turf that costs 10p per square metre?
8. Here is a sketch of the floor of a room.
   (a) What is the area of the room?
   A carpet is laid on the floor.
   (b) What is the area of the carpet?

   The carpet does not cover all of the floor.
   (c) How much of the floor is not covered?

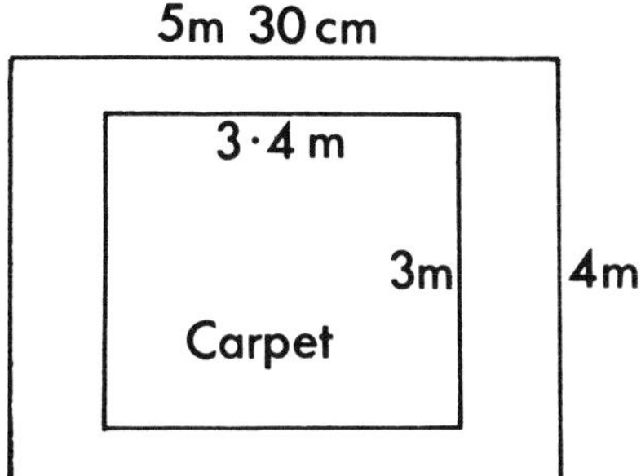

9. A carpet 4 metres long and 2 metres 60 centimetres wide is laid on the floor of a room 5 metres 80 centimetres long and 4 metres wide. How much of the floor is not carpeted? A sketch will help.
10. A rectangular lawn, 17 m by 11 m, is to be laid with a rose bed, 5 m by 3 m, in the centre. How much turf will be needed?

On a paint tin it is stated that one litre is enough for 20 square metres. The walls on each side of a corridor, 21 metres long and 260 cm high, are to receive two coats of paint.

11. What is the total area of the two walls?
12. How many litres of paint must be ordered by the decorator to make sure he has enough to complete the job?
13. What will the paint cost at £2·50 per 5 litres?
14. A clock chimes at each quarter-hour interval. How often are the chimes heard from 2 p.m. to 4 p.m., inclusive?

Pocket Money

Write answers only:

1. If Bob bought a tenpenny saving stamp each week how much would he save in one full year?
2. How soon can I save £2 at the rate of 10p per week?
3. How soon can I save £4 at the rate of 20p per week?
4. Roy's father promised to add five pence to each ten pence that was saved towards buying a new bicycle. How much should his father add when Roy had saved £8?
5. Out of her fifty pence per week pocket money Sheila had to pay 1p bus fare each way to and from school and five pence dinner money per day. How much money did she have to spend as she liked in a normal school week?
6. When Rita received her pocket money of 40p she still had left from the previous week a ten, three fives, two twos and four pennies. What was the new total amount?
7. Bob had saved 84p when he bought three handkerchiefs at 15p each for Father's birthday. How much was left?
8. Roy helped in a shop on Saturdays from 9 a.m. to 12.30 p.m. If he was paid 15p per hour how much did he earn?
9. Sheila helped in a shop on Saturdays from 12.30 p.m. to 4.30 p.m. If she was paid 18p per hour how much did she receive?
10. Roy had saved some pocket money to spend at the annual fair. He had a fifty, three tens, five fives and three twos. What was the total?
11. Bob had £1·42 saved when it was the annual fair, but he needed 9p for bus fares and 30p for a visit to the cinema and other items. How much could he spend at the fair?
12. Rita saved 83 twos in a vase to pay for gramophone records. Was that enough to pay for a record at £1·70?
13. It took Roy six weeks to save £1. How long should it take him to save £2·50?
14. Bob received 80p each week for delivering newspapers. If he saved half, how long did it take him to save £2?

1. A lorry set out with a load of 80 bags of cement. What part of the load remains after 60 bags have been delivered?
2. An empty jug weighed 348 g. When containing $\frac{1}{2}$ litre of milk it weighed 866 g. What was the weight of 1 litre of milk?
3. What is the total thickness in centimetres when three pieces of wood, measuring 16 mm, 12 mm and 8 mm respectively, are fixed together?

4. Mother had 1 kg 240 g of beef for Friday, and 1 kg 710 g for Sunday. Find (a) the total weight, (b) the cost at 52p per kg.
5. What must be added to a beam 125 mm thick so that it exactly fits a space 155 mm wide?
6. An alloy has to contain $\frac{1}{2}$ of its weight of copper, $\frac{1}{3}$ of tin and the rest of zinc. What part must be of zinc?

Here is a ring having an outside diameter of 17·4 cm and an inside diameter of 15·7 cm.

7. What is the radius of the inner circle?
8. What is the radius of the outer circle?
9. What is the thickness of the ring?
10. Find the perimeter of a triangle having sides of 7·8 cm, 10·5 cm and 5 cm.

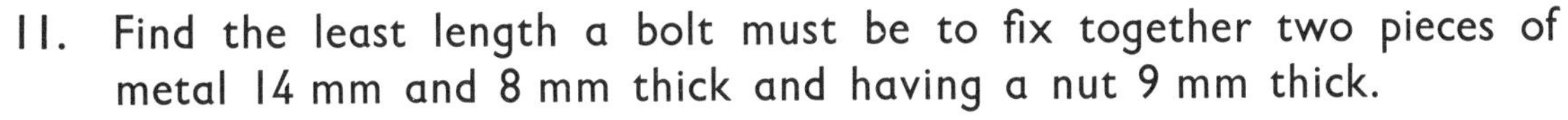

11. Find the least length a bolt must be to fix together two pieces of metal 14 mm and 8 mm thick and having a nut 9 mm thick.
12. By how much is $3\frac{7}{8}$ gross less than $5\frac{1}{4}$ gross?
13. Find the time needed to pack a box, allowing $6\frac{1}{2}$ sec. to arrange the contents, $3\frac{1}{3}$ sec. to fix the lid and $4\frac{1}{4}$ sec. to label it.

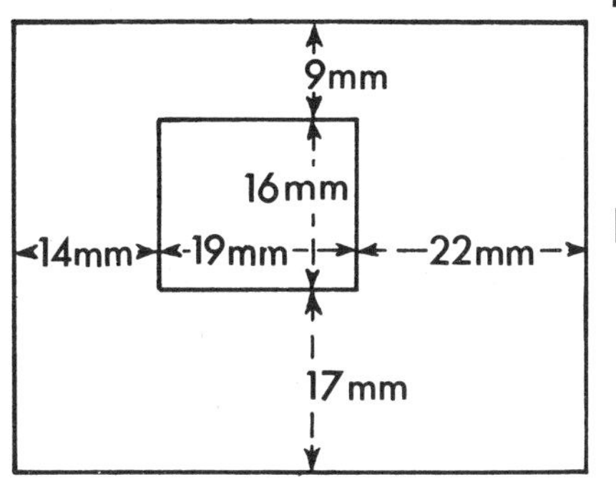

14. Find what must be the length and breadth of a piece of metal that will exactly allow a centre piece to be cut as shown in the diagram.
15. What would be the length of the sides of a square sheet of metal that would allow to be cut from the centre a square with sides of 37 mm set 22 mm from the outer edges?

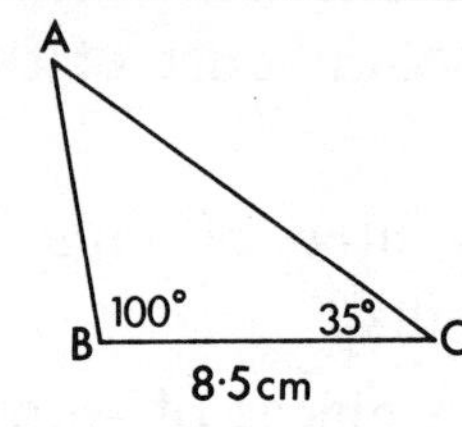

1. Draw a triangle as shown in the sketch.
2. Find the lengths of sides AB and AC.
3. Find the angle BAC.
4. What is the total of all three angles?
5. Draw a right angle EFG having sides EF 12·6 cm and FG 9·8 cm. Join the ends to make a triangle. Measure ∠GEF and ∠FGE.
6. What are the lengths of EG and GF?

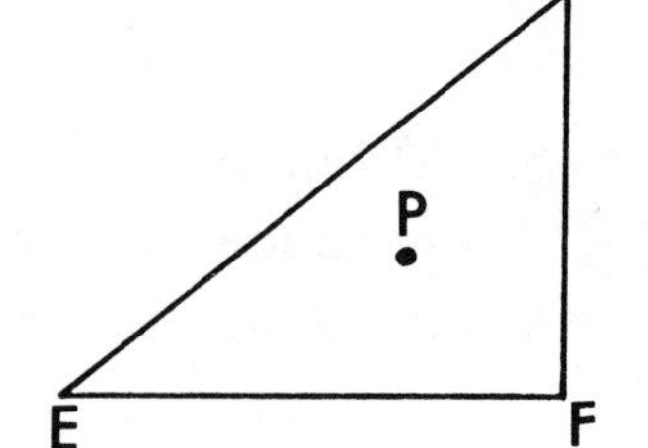

7. What is the total of all angles in any triangle?
8. In your triangle GEF make a dot near the centre and put the letter P. Measure the angles at P:
   ∠EPF   ∠EPG   ∠GPF
9. What is the total of the three angles at P?
10. Draw a square having sides 7·4 cm. Letter the sides KLMN.
11. Draw the diagonals. Put the letter R where the diagonals cross.
12. How many sides to your shape? How many angles at the centre?
13. What is the total of ∠KRN, ∠KRL, ∠LRM, and ∠MRN?

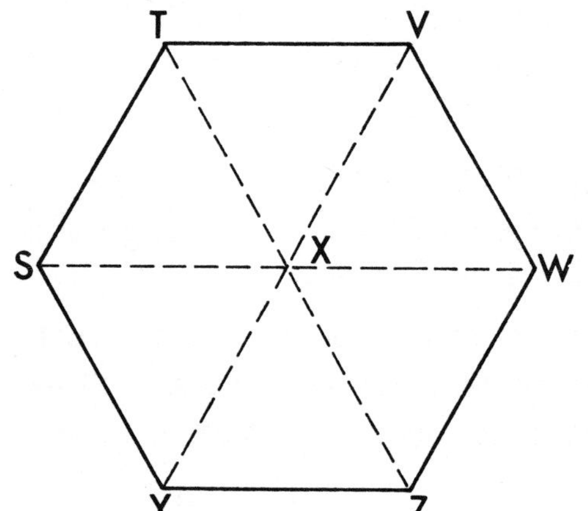

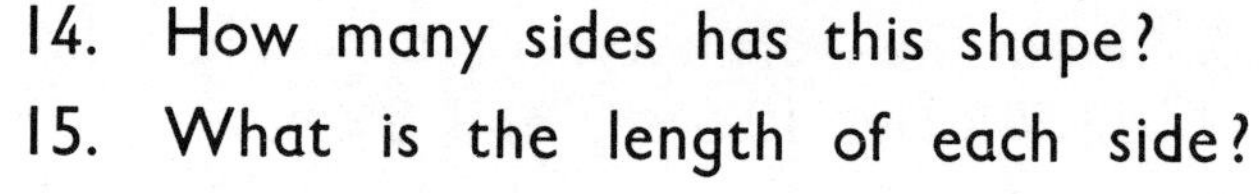

14. How many sides has this shape?
15. What is the length of each side?

It is called a regular hexagon.

16. Find ∠YXZ and ∠ZXW.

17. Guess ∠VXT and ∠TXS.
18. What is the total of the angles at X?
19. Find ∠SYX and ∠XSY.
20. What can you say about the angles of △TXS?
21. What can you say about the sides of △TXS?
22. Do more measuring in this way then write all you can about a regular hexagon and equilateral triangles.

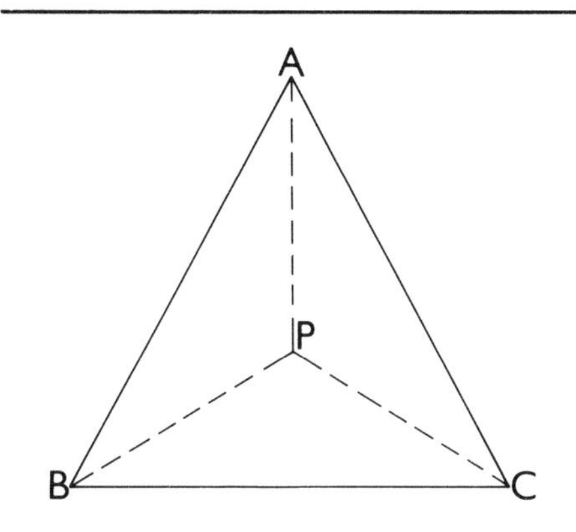

Here is an equilateral triangle. As it has all sides equal we say it is a regular figure or shape.

1. Is the square a regular shape?

P is the centre point of the triangle.

2. Find the size of each angle at P.
3. Find the total of the angles at P.
4. Were all angles equal at P in the right angled triangle?
5. What was their total?
6. What can you say about the sides BP and PA of △ABP?

It is an ISOSCELES triangle.

7. Name 2 more isosceles triangles.

Here is a regular pentagon.
∠ABC, ∠BCD, etc. are INTERIOR angles.
By continuing CD to R we make an EXTERIOR angle. Another is ∠SEA.

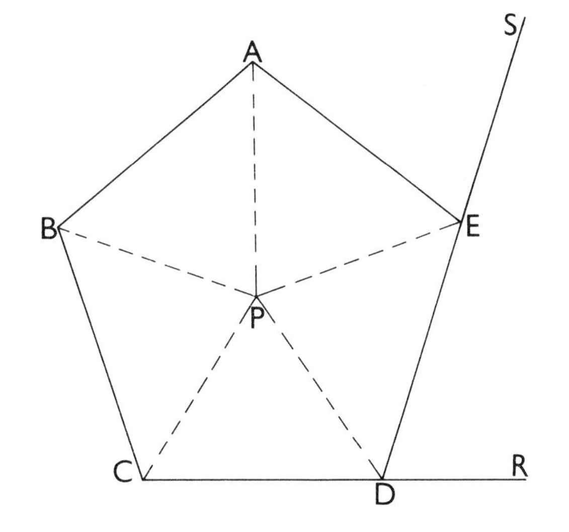

8. Measure all exterior angles.
9. What is their total?
10. What is the total of angles at P?
11. Divide 360° by the number of sides.
12. What kind of triangles are in a regular pentagon?
13. Copy this table and complete it.

Regular polygon	Total of centre angles	Number of sides	Angle at centre	Exterior angle	Interior angle
Triangle					
Square					
Hexagon					
Pentagon					
Octagon					

14. Write anything else you can discover about regular polygons.

1. How many pieces of ribbon, each 25 centimetres long, can you cut from one metre of ribbon?
2. How many pieces of string, each 40 centimetres long, can you cut from six metres of string?
3. How many ribbons 35 cm long can be cut from $10\frac{1}{2}$ metres of ribbon?
4. Two and a half kilogrammes of tobacco are made up into 50 gramme packets. How many packets should there be?
5. A metric ton of poultry food is weighed out into $2\frac{1}{2}$ kg bags. How many bags should there be?
6. How long will it take to save £3 if you can save twenty-five pence weekly?
7. How many books at 36p each can be bought with £1·80?
8. If a group of men can make one motor tyre every six minutes how many tyres will they make in two hours?
9. If another type of tyre can be made in twelve mnutes how many tyres can be made in three hours?
10. A new car leaves a factory every fifteen minutes. How many should be completed between 9 a.m. and 11.30 a.m.?
11. The rental for a wireless set was 43p per week. For how many weeks had it been rented when the charge was £7·31?
12. How many fifteen centimetre tiles will it take in each row along a wall which is 12·6 m long?
13. On the outside of a carton it states that the total weight of biscuits enclosed is 17 kg. If the biscuits are in 340 gramme packets, how many packets are there in the carton?
14. It is agreed to spend £5·25 on cakes for a school party. How many cakes at $2\frac{1}{2}$p each can be bought with that amount?
15. For school dinners it usually takes 125 kg of potatoes per day. For how many days will three tons of potatoes last?

If it took Walter, aged eight, 5 minutes to cycle 1 kilometre, would he cycle 100 km in 8 hours 20 minutes?

When a plan is made so that all the numbers in a list follow each other in the same way, we say that those numbers are in series.

The plan in each of the following series is to add the same amount to each number to make the one after it. Find the plan and say what should be the next number in each series.

1. 1, 3, 5, 7, 9,.. .. 20, 25, 30, 35,.. ..
2. 0, 3, 6, 9, 12,.. .. 31, 38, 45, 52, 59,.. ..
3. $\frac{1}{4}$, $\frac{1}{2}$, $\frac{3}{4}$, 1,.. .. $\frac{1}{8}$, $\frac{1}{4}$, $\frac{3}{8}$, $\frac{1}{2}$, $\frac{5}{8}$,.. ..

The plan in each of the following series is to take from each number the same amount to make the one after it. Find the plan and say what should be the next number in each series.

4. 12, 10, 8, 6, 4,.. .. 60, 57, 54, 51,.. ..
5. 73, 63, 53, 43,.. .. 91, 85, 79, 73, 67,.. ..
6. 2, $1\frac{3}{4}$, $1\frac{1}{2}$, $1\frac{1}{4}$,.. .. 1, $\frac{11}{12}$, $\frac{5}{6}$, $\frac{3}{4}$, $\frac{2}{3}$, $\frac{7}{12}$,.. ..

The plan in each of the following series of numbers is found when you subtract the first from the second, the second from the third, the third from the fourth and so on. Find the plan and give the next number in the series.

7. 1, 2, 4, 7, 11, 16,.. .. 2, 4, 7, 9, 12, 14,.. ..
8. 0, 1, 2, 4, 5, 6, 8,.. .. $\frac{1}{8}$, $\frac{1}{4}$, $\frac{1}{2}$, $\frac{5}{8}$, $\frac{7}{8}$, 1,.. ..

The following series use all the plans above. Find the plan for each series and give the next item.

9. 1, $1\frac{1}{2}$, 2, $2\frac{1}{2}$, 3,.. .. 17, 15, 13, 11, 9,.. ..
10. $\frac{1}{3}$, 1, $1\frac{2}{3}$, $2\frac{1}{3}$, 3,.. .. 7, 8, 11, 12, 15, 16,.. ..
11. 1, $\frac{15}{16}$, $\frac{7}{8}$, $\frac{13}{16}$, $\frac{3}{4}$,.. .. $\frac{1}{10}$, $\frac{3}{10}$, $\frac{2}{5}$, $\frac{3}{5}$, $\frac{7}{10}$, $\frac{9}{10}$,.. ..
12. 7 mm, 1·3 cm, 1·9 cm, 2·5 cm,.. ..
13. 61p, 70p, 80p, 91p,.. .. 1·75 l, 1·5 l, 1·25 l, 1 l,.. ..
14. 1 min. 25 sec., 1 min. 50 sec., 2 min. 15 sec.,.. ..
15. 100, 88, 79, 67, 58,.. .. $\frac{1}{4}$, $\frac{3}{8}$, $\frac{5}{8}$, $\frac{3}{4}$, 1, $1\frac{1}{8}$,.. ..

Lines

Here are eight groups of lines. Use the letters from these groups to answer the questions below them.

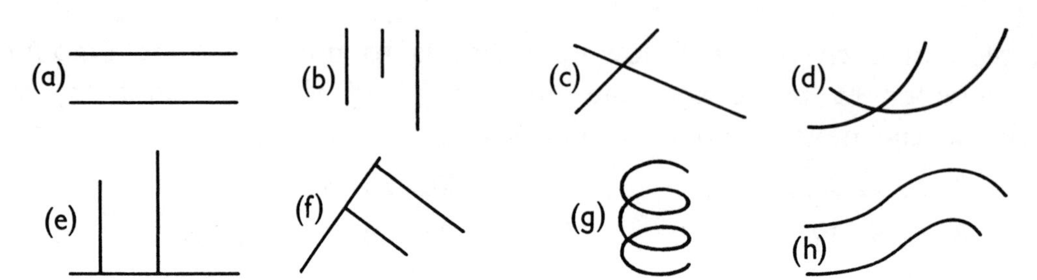

1. State which groups contain lines that are:
   (a) straight and intersect
   (b) horizontal and parallel
   (c) vertical and parallel
   (d) perpendicular but not vertical
   (e) vertical and perpendicular
   (f) curved and parallel
   (g) curved and intersect
   (h) curved and spiral

2. Measure the lengths of these two lines.

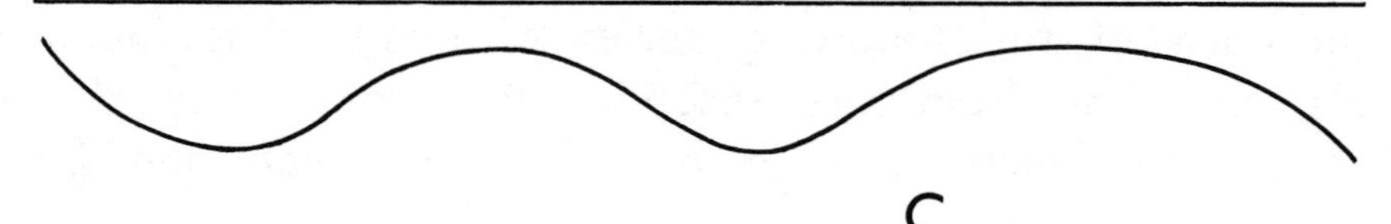

3. Which of these lines are:
   (a) vertical?
   (b) perpendicular to each other?
   (c) horizontal?
   (d) parallel to each other?
   (e) slanting?

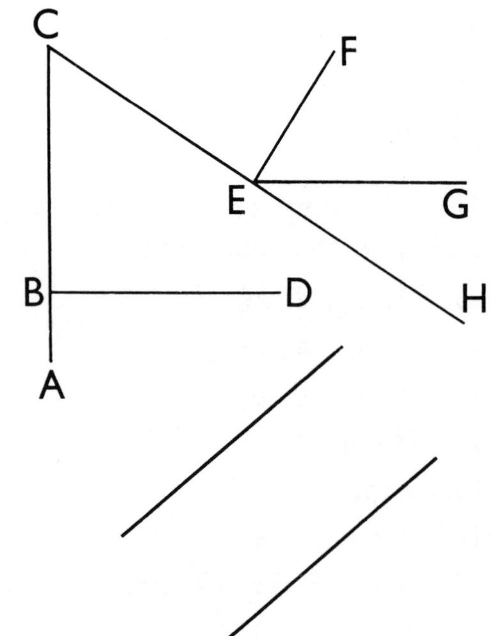

4. Here are two parallel lines. Find the following distances between them:
   (a) the perpendicular;
   (b) the vertical;
   (c) the horizontal.

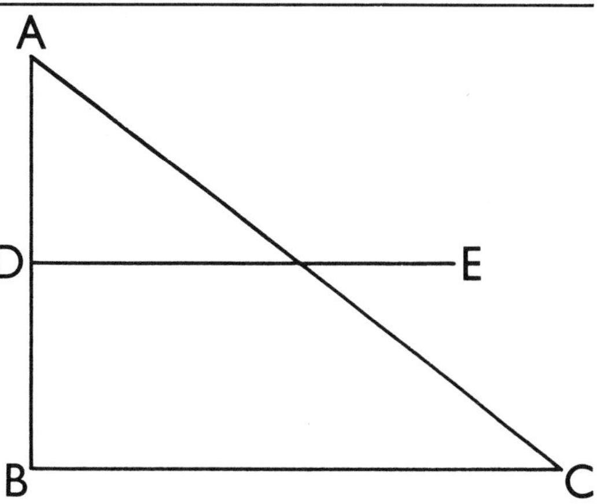

1. Draw a triangle as shown on the right, making BC 12·7 cm, angle ABC 90° and AB 9·5 cm. Find the length of AC.
2. Mark the point D, which is the middle point of AB, and draw DE parallel to BC.
3. Measure from A and from C to where DE cuts AC. What does DE do to AC?

Draw a vertical line 5·7 cm long. Letter it PK. At P draw a horizontal line PO 12 cm. At K draw a line KM 4·4 cm in the same direction as PO and parallel to it. Join M to O.

4. How long is MO?

Draw and cut out a rectangle 15·2 cm by 11·4 cm. Draw both diagonals.

5. Find (a) the perimeter, (b) the area.
6. What are the lengths of the diagonals?

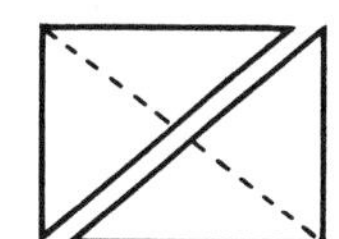

Cut along one diagonal and form the pieces into a triangle.

7. What is the area of this triangle?
8. Measure the base of the triangle and its height, then multiply the two together.
9. What relation has your answer to the area?
10. Find the perimeter of this triangle.

Cut along the other diagonal passing through each of your two triangles so that four triangles are formed. Arrange these four triangles into two diamond shapes.

11. Measure the diagonals and the lengths of the sides of each new shape. Say what relationship they bear to each other.

Re-arrange your pieces to form a parallelogram.

12. What is the area of the parallelogram?
13. What is the length of (a) the long side, (b) the short side?
14. Find the perimeter of the parallelogram.

Average

Find the average of each of these groups:

1. 7, 9, 8, 9, 7. 27, 30, 36, 43. 182, 309, 290, 178, 96.

2. $23\frac{1}{2}$p, 20p, 15p, $19\frac{1}{2}$p. 1 kg 200 g, 700 g, 1 kg 850 g.

Find the average of each of these groups, giving the answer to the nearest whole number.

3.

		litres	m	cm	£
46	306	15·72	3	42	3·95
43	176	9·6		85	1·48
72	89	7·08	1	8	0·89
9	508	10·56		67	1·06
58	64				
36					

Here are the temperatures taken at three points in a school to test a new boiler measured in degrees celsius.

Room	8 a.m.	11 a.m.	2 p.m.	4 p.m.
A	16	16	17	16·5
B	16·5	18	17	17·5
C	16·5	16·5	18·5	18·5

4. Find the average daily temperature recorded for each of the three rooms to the nearest whole degree.

Here are some interesting results from using averages:

5. Work out these results to complete the last three columns, taking each average to the nearest whole number.

	English			Arithc.		General Subjects			Total Marks	Average Mark	Group Position
	1	2	3	1	2	Hist.	Geog.	Nat.			
A	74	62	58	78	88	61	76	78			
B	70	73	62	83	81	72	69	70			
C	77	83	79	69	71	68	68	74			

6. On a walking holiday a group of youths covered the following distances on succeeding days: 18 km, $17\frac{1}{2}$ km, $18\frac{1}{2}$ km, 15 km, $16\frac{1}{2}$ km, and $19\frac{1}{2}$ km. What was the average distance per day?

Averages

1. Find the average of 3 consecutive numbers the first of which is 4.
2. Find three consecutive numbers. Their average is 9.
3. The sum of three consecutive numbers is 192. Find them.
4. The sum of three consecutive even numbers is 18. Find them.
5. The average of five consecutive odd numbers is 35. What are the numbers?
6. A new school has 12 class-rooms and it is built to average 32 pupils per class. What is the highest number of pupils the school should take?
7. At the grocer's a head teacher found that eating apples averaged 5 per $\frac{1}{2}$ kg. How many kilogrammes of apples should be ordered so that each of 187 pupils can have one apple each?
8. If a man can average £17·84 for his weekly wage what should he earn in 10 weeks?
9. A gardener hopes to average a yield of twenty times the weight of seed potatoes planted. If he plants 60 kg of seed potatoes what does he estimate will be the weight of his crop in tons?
10. Find to the nearest month the average age of a group of children of whom 1 is 9 yr. 10 mth., 2 are 10 yr. 2 mth. and 3 are 10 yr. 5 mth.
11. Two drivers set off with a large van from Worcester to Edinburgh, a total of 500 km. They hope to average 40 km per h. (a) How long should the journey take? (b) Leaving Worcester at 8.30 a.m. at what time should they arrive in Edinburgh?
12. What is the approximate weight of two gross of eggs if the average weight of the eggs is 57 grammes?
13. Ted averaged $37\frac{1}{2}$p per day during Scouts' week. How much from Monday to Saturday, inclusive?
14. In a Freedom from Hunger Week four girls set out to raise money by making and selling glove puppets at $12\frac{1}{2}$p. They agreed to average two each daily from Monday to Friday inclusive. How much did they hope to raise?

1. A plantation of two thousand four hundred and sixty trees is to be increased by seven hundred and ninety trees. What will be the total number of trees in the plantation?
2. Of two thousand five hundred eggs, two thousand four hundred and six were sound. How many eggs were broken?

Here are some totals, in thousands, of population figures for the countries within the United Kingdom, rounded to the nearest thousand.

Year	England and Wales	Scotland	Northern Ireland	Total	Increase
1962	46 709	5 197	1 435		
1963	47 028	5 205	1 446		
1964	47 401	5 206	1 458		
1965	47 763	5 204	1 469		
1966	48 075	5 191	1 478		
1967	48 391	5 187	1 491		

3. Was there an increase during each twelve-month period for each section of the United Kingdom?
4. Find the figures to complete the last two columns of the table.
5. In which year did the figures show the greatest increase?
6. In which year did the figures show the least increase?
7. What was the over-all increase from 1962 to 1967?
8. State in words the actual number of the population of the United Kingdom calculated to the nearest thousand for 1967.

During a period of 13 weeks regular work 58 201 metric tons of coal were produced at a colliery. The average number of days worked per week was 5 and the average number of men employed was 407.

9. Find the average output during that period for one week.
10. Find the average output per day for that colliery.
11. Find the average output per man per day.

1. How much is left when 78·25 tons is taken from 100 tons?
2. What is the total of 0·34 hr, 0·62 hr and 0·4 hr?

Here are some examples of how decimals are used.
(Temperatures are daily averages—Sunshine is daily average for each month and centigrade degrees are equal to celsius degrees.)

Month	England and Wales				Scotland			
	Temperature Centigrade		Sunshine hours		Temperature Centigrade		Sunshine hours	
	1967	1968	1967	1968	1967	1968	1967	1968
January	5·0°	5·0°	2·0	1·2	4·5°	3·9°	1·3	1·1
February	6·1°	2·8°	2·8	2·2	5·8°	2·3°	2·2	2·7
March	7·7°	7·0°	5·0	4·0	6·0°	5·6°	3·5	2·9
April	8·3°	8·5°	4·2	5·9	7·5°	7·1°	4·7	5·3
May	10·8°	10·3°	5·2	5·0	9·0°	8·3°	4·9	4·7
June	14·5°	14·9°	7·1	6·3	12·8°	13·2°	6·9	6·3

The following questions refer to these tables, i.e. the first half of each of the years 1967 and 1968.

3. Find the coldest month in 1968 in England and Wales.
4. Find the sunniest month in 1968 in England and Wales.
5. Which was the coldest month in 1967 in Scotland?
6. Which was the coldest month in 1968 in Scotland?
7. How much more sunshine was there in England and Wales during June '67 than in June '68?
8. What was the difference between the minimum and maximum average temperatures for the first half of 1968 in Scotland?
9. Find the average daily amount of sunshine in England and Wales during the months of April, May and June in 1968.
10. The average daily hours of sunshine for the whole of 1967 in Scotland was 3·4. Find how much above or below this was the daily average for the half-year shown.
11. Look at the figures for the month of June. Can one say that the highest number of hours of sunshine produced the highest average temperature when you compare the figures for 1967 with those for 1968?

Decimals in Problems

1. By how much is line A less than line B? Give your answer as a fraction and as a decimal in centimetres.
   A —————————— B ————————————
2. By how much is line C greater than line D? Give your answer as a fraction and as a decimal in centimetres.
   C ———————————————— D ——————————————
3. Which is the greater, 0·5 of 50p or $\frac{1}{5}$ of £1?
4. What is the total thickness when a sheet of plywood 1·3 cm thick is fixed to another sheet which is 1·8 centimetre thick?
5. How much must be removed from a steel bar one cm thick in order for it to fit into a groove 0·7 cm wide?
6. A slot is 2·5 mm wide. Which of these thicknesses of material would pass easily through the slot?
   $\frac{1}{2}$ cm, 0·2 cm, 0·18 cm, 0·022 m
7. How many pence equal 0·2 of £1?
8. How many kilogrammes equal 0·1 of one ton?
9. Which of these sizes of sheet metal would best fit a groove which is $\frac{1}{2}$ cm wide: 7·5 mm, 2·5 mm, 0·6 mm, 5 mm?
10. Write what is:

0·1 of 10 pence	0·1 of £1	0·1 of 1 ton
0·2 of 50 pence	0·6 of £1	0·7 of 1 ton
0·2 of 1 hour	0·7 of 1 hour	0·4 of $\frac{1}{2}$ hour
0·75 of 1 metre	0·75 of 1 min.	0·5 of $\frac{1}{4}$ hour
0·25 of 1 hour	0·3 of 30 days	0·01 of 1 m

11. Records, in thousand metric tons, show that during December 1967 the amount of beef produced in Great Britain was 61·7 and in December 1968 the amount was 63·4. Find what was the increase in tons.

12. An Ayrshire cow averages 3·88 grammes of butterfat per 100 grammes of milk, whereas a Guernsey cow averages 4·56 grammes. What is the average increase of the Guernsey cow over the Ayrshire cow for each kilogramme of milk produced?
13. It is found that Freisian cows average 3·69 g of butterfat per 100 grammes of milk and Shorthorn cows average 3·62 g. What should be the average weight of butterfat per kilogramme of milk if a farmer mixes 200 kg of milk from his Shorthorns with 300 kg from his Freisians?

Revision

Write answers only:

1. Tom is 18 years old and John is 5 years older. How old will John be in a year's time?
2. A pencil and pen together cost 9p. Find the cost of the pen if it cost a five more than the pencil.
3. If you paid for some twopenny stamps with a ten and a five, how many stamps did you buy?
4. If May 4th is on Sunday on which day is May 12th?
5. Find the total weight of 7 parcels, each weighing 650 g.
6. By what number must I multiply 2·8 in order to give the digit 8 the same place value as the digit 6 in 360·7?
7. What should be the next number in this series? 0, 1, 3, 6, 10,.. ..
8. Find Jim's average score if in three cricket matches he made 8, 27 and 13 runs.
9. What would be the area of a square with sides of 5 metres?

Work in your book:

10. What weight should be left in a truck which contained 11 metric tons 200 kg of coal after 132 fifty-kilogramme bags have been filled?
11. At a hotel 15 l of milk are used on Monday, 19·5 l on Tuesday, 14·5 l on Wednesday and on Thursday, and 11 l on Friday. What is the daily average?
12. How much can Bill save in one year if each week he saves one-fifth from his pocket money of 65p?
13. What distance on a scale 2 cm=5 km is represented by this line?

    ---

14. What will be the cost at 20p per 1000 sq. cm of fixing a new plastic top to a table that is 150 cm long and 120 cm wide?
15. If a train travels at an average speed of 45 km/h how far should it have gone between 10.30 a.m. and 2.50 p.m.?
16. Find (a) the perimeter, and (b) the area of a rectangle that is 105 cm wide and 180 cm long.
17. How much material would be left from 9 m if a mother used 2·5 m, 2·75 m and 3·25 m of it to make frocks for her 3 daughters?

Three Dimensions

These are all flat shapes or two dimensional shapes.

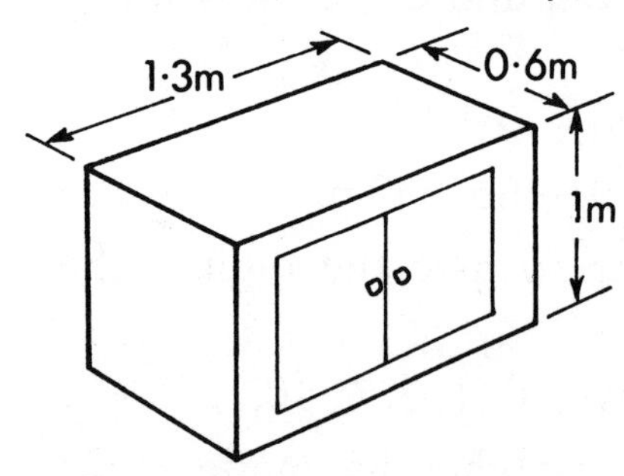

Here is a three dimensional shape.

1. State the following measurements of the cupboard.
   height width depth

On page 18 you made a cone from a circle. You created a third dimension—height as well as the circle at the base.

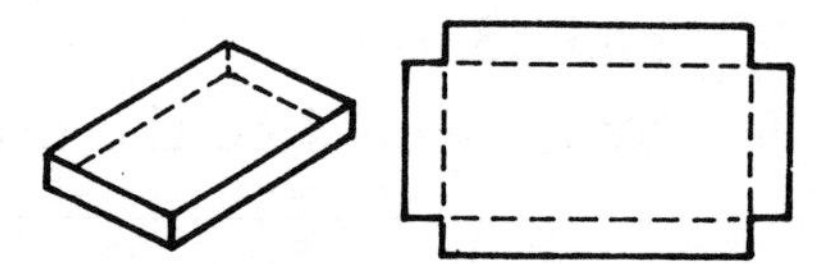

2. Obtain the empty tray of a match box. Notice it has depth as well as width and length.
   Carefully cut down the corners of the tray so that the sides can be pressed flat on your desk. You have reduced a three dimensional shape to a two dimensional shape.

Let us do the reverse.

3. On strong paper or thin card draw the following shape to the given dimensions.

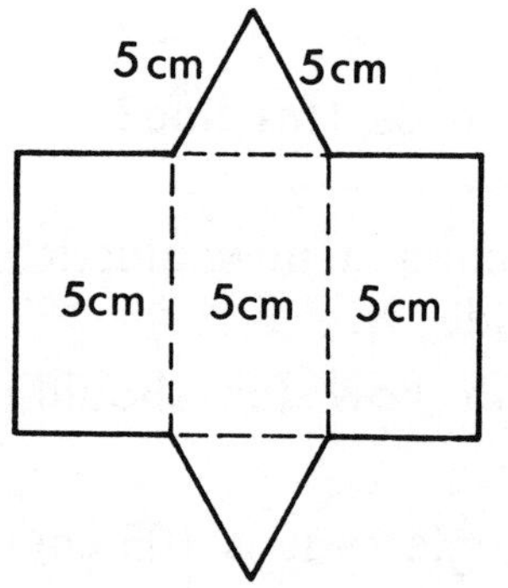

4. Crease along the dotted lines so that the triangular shapes rise in the same manner at right angles to the centre panel, and the two outer rectangular panels rise up to fit along the edges of the triangles.
5. Fix your shape with cellotape.
   You have a TRIANGULAR PRISM.
6. How many faces has your triangular prism?
7. How many edges has your triangular prism?

Here are dimensions to make 2 more triangular prisms.

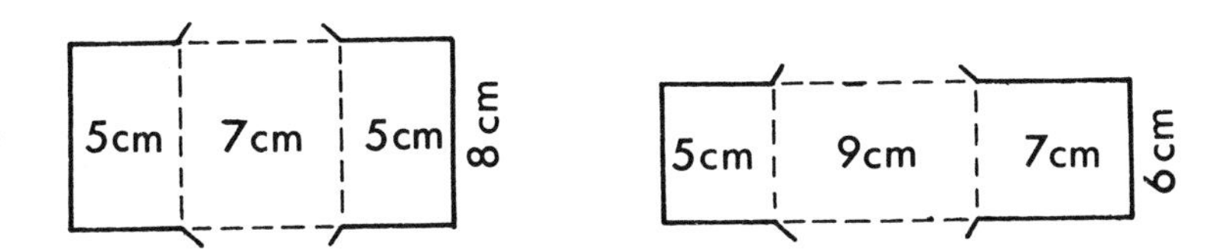

1. Work out the size of the triangular ends and make your drawing.
2. Cut out your shapes and fix the edges that meet.
3. Examine all your prisms as they stand on ends and on different sides.

So far our prisms have three sides. Here are dimensions for making prisms with four sides.

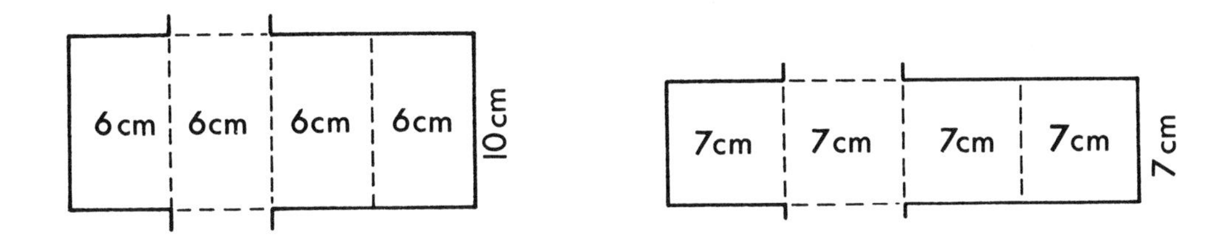

4. Again work out the sizes and shapes of the ends. What is the shape?
5. Draw your shapes, cut them out and make your prisms.
6. Stand your two rectangular prisms on the ends and on the sides. Examine them carefully and note how they differ.
7. What is special about the last prism?

We call it a CUBE.

8. Draw the shape, cut out and construct a rectangular prism 12 cm high and having one pair of opposite sides 7 cm wide and the other opposite pair 9 cm wide.
9. Draw the shape, cut out and construct a cube having its faces 6 centimetres wide.

Costs

Water to a farm has to pass through a meter and is charged for at the rate of 15p for each complete kilolitre. The meter reading in March was 423·105 kl and in June 916·891 kl.

1. How many kilolitres had been used in that period?
2. For how many kilolitres would be the charge up to March?
3. How many kilolitres would be charged for from March to June?
4. What was the charge for water used from March to June?

The fare from London to Washington by air is £185 single and £334·25 return. Children below the age of 12 go for half fare.

5. What is saved by booking a return journey instead of a single each way?
6. What will be the total single fare for a husband, his wife, a son of 12 and a daughter of 7?
7. What will be the total return fare for a mother, twins aged 3 and a son of 10?

Here is part of a table showing the costs of carpet at various sizes.

Length in metres	Width in metres				
	1	$1\frac{1}{2}$	2	$2\frac{1}{2}$	3
2	£3·97	£6·35	£8·39	£10·70	£12·89
$2\frac{1}{4}$	£4·99	£7·50	£10·20	£11·99	£14·78
$2\frac{1}{2}$	£5·88	£8·67	£11·45	£13·90	£16·20
$2\frac{3}{4}$	£6·29	£9·48	£12·79	£15·50	£18·25
3	£7·39	£10·99	£14·65	£17·90	£21·95
$3\frac{1}{2}$	£8·75	£12·99	£17·70	£20·90	£26·90

8. State what would be the cost of carpets having measurements of:
   (a) $2\frac{1}{4}$ m by 1 m (b) $3\frac{1}{2}$ m by 3 m
   (c) $2\frac{1}{2}$ m by $1\frac{1}{2}$ m (d) A $2\frac{1}{2}$ m square
   (e) A 3 m square (f) $2\frac{3}{4}$ m by $2\frac{1}{2}$ m

The charge for electricity on a bill is given as 3p per unit for the first 72 units and 1p per unit for the rest. State what should be the charge for:

9. (a) 100 units (b) 276 units
   (c) twice the number of units in (b)

Sometimes it is necessary to make records of classroom temperatures to check if the heating and ventilating systems are working as they should do. One way of doing it could be pictorially, representing the temperatures by drawings of the thermometer, and then placing besides each drawing the figures for the reading, as shown below:

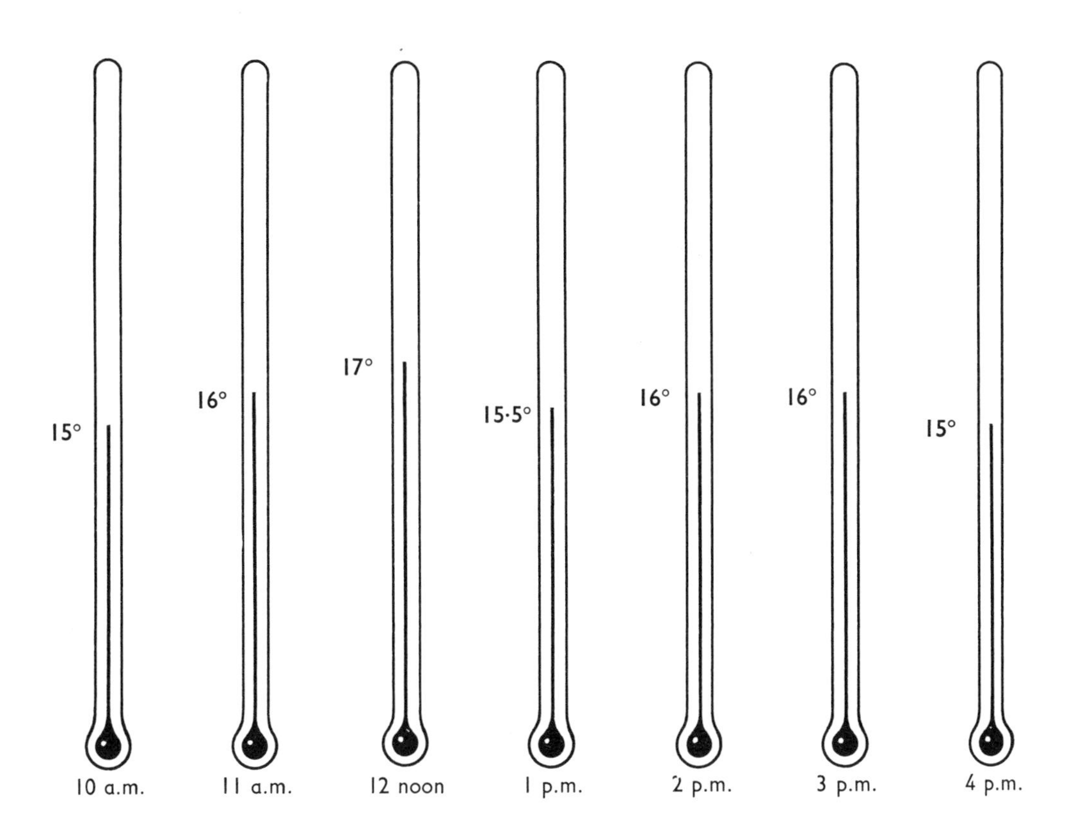

1. At what intervals have the readings been taken?
2. What was the temperature at 11 a.m.?
3. At what time was the highest reading taken?
4. At what time was the lowest reading taken?
5. At what time was the biggest drop in temperature recorded?

A Graph

Look back at the diagram on the previous page. What one really does is look at the first temperature, 15°C, and then allow one's eyes to travel across the page from that point, noting how the temperature rises or falls. This can be done quicker and more effectively by a line. A sheet of paper is marked off as for a histogram, with temperatures marked on the left and hourly time intervals marked along the base line. Instead of columns we move up the left-hand temperature line to put a dot to correspond with the reading on the thermometer at 10 a.m. At 11 a.m. we move up the line representing that point until we come to the temperature level, and again put a dot, so that across the paper we finish with a series of dots to correspond to the tops of the alcohol levels in the thermometers. By joining these dots with a line a quick glance tells us when there were changes.

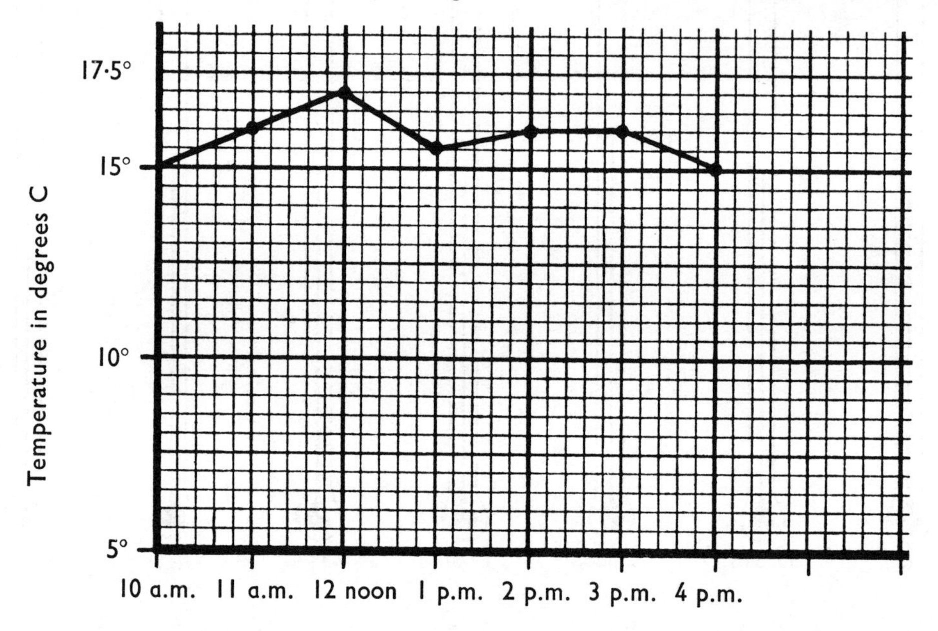

1. Between what times was the biggest fall?
2. Was there a rise in temperature as quick as that fall?
3. At which part of the day was temperature maintained at a fairly steady level?
4. Make a graph to show outside temperatures taken hourly throughout one school day.

A Temperature Graph

Here is a graph which enables us to convert temperatures from Fahrenheit to Celsius or Celsius to Fahrenheit.

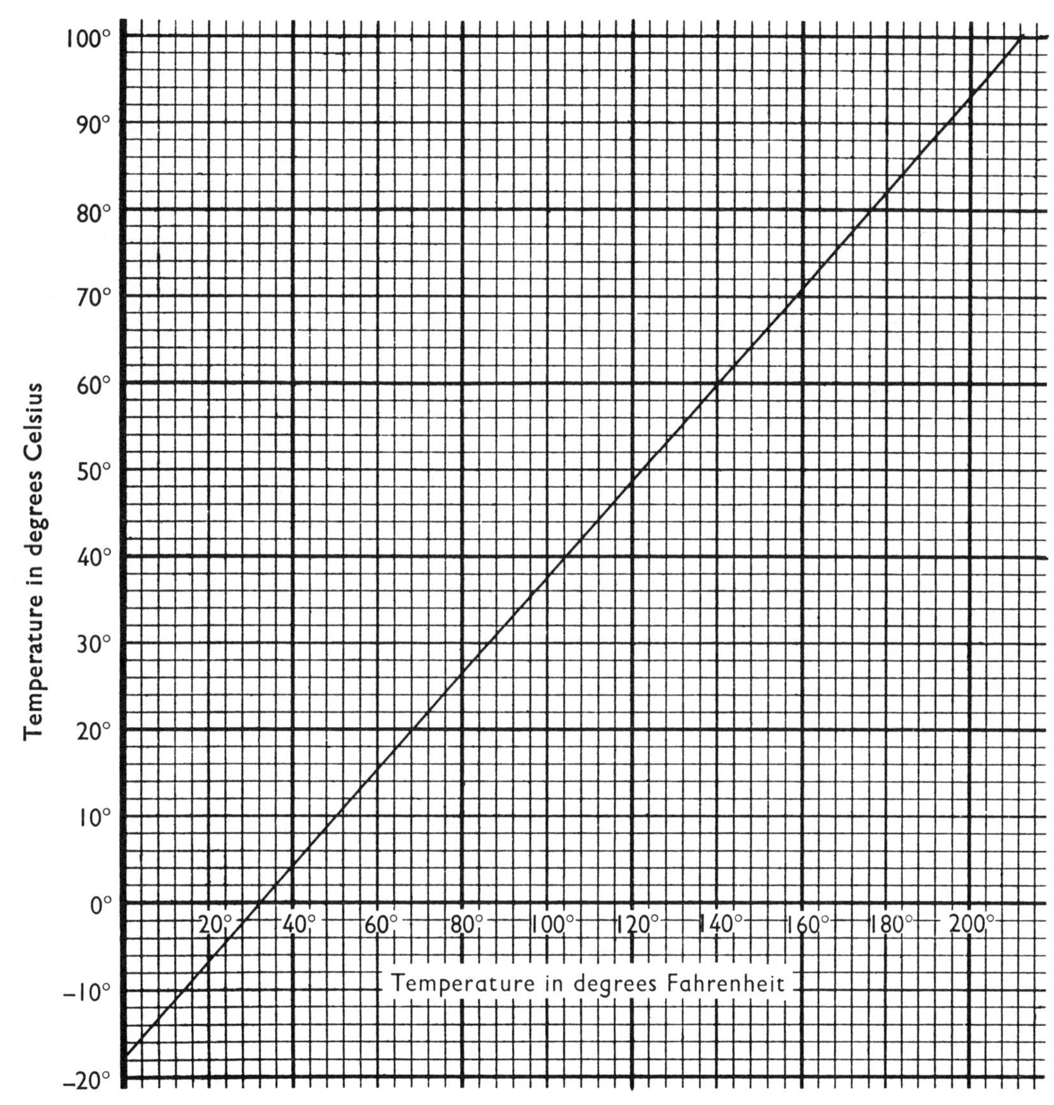

1. How many degrees Celsius are represented by one square?
2. How many degrees Fahrenheit are represented by one square?
3. Give to the nearest whole number, degrees Celsius equal to:
   80°F 144°F 180°F 32°F 212°F
4. Give, to the nearest whole number, degrees Fahrenheit equal to:
   7°C 32°C 64°C 80°C 100°C

A Line Graph

Here a curved line connects all points which represent pairs of numbers which can be multiplied together to make 48.

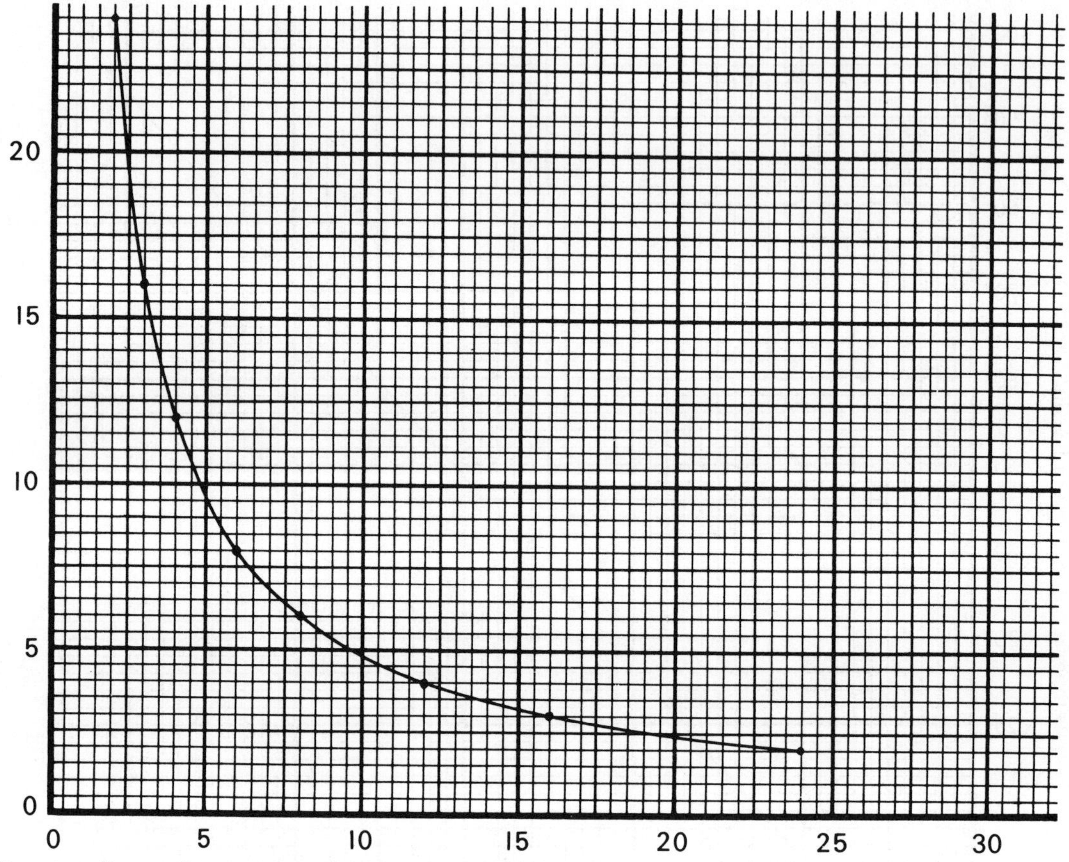

Pairs of numbers whose products = 48

1. Cut out the 7 rectangles which have an area of 48 square centimetres (omit 48 × 1, 1 × 48) and arrange them to give the effect of a graph.
2. Which number multiplied by 12 makes 48?
3. What is the length of a rectangle having an area of 48 square metres and its width 8 metres?
4. What is the width of a rectangle having an area of 48 square kilometres and a length of 16 kilometres?
5. Use the graph to find the approximate lengths of the other sides of rectangles having an area of 48 square metres if the other sides are
   11 metres   19 metres   14 metres $4\frac{1}{2}$ metres
6. Draw 3 similar graphs to connect points which represent all pairs of numbers which multiplied together make 36, 60 and 96.

At the Sales

1. A lady paid for a hat costing $99\frac{1}{2}$p with a fifty, four tens and two fives. How much was the change?
2. A young man bought for £9·97$\frac{1}{2}$ a coat that had been priced at 12 pounds. How much had he saved?
3. Mother needed $3\frac{1}{2}$ metres of cloth to make a frock for Jean. It was to cost 39p per yard. What did Mother save by buying a remnant of $3\frac{3}{4}$ m of the same material for $99\frac{1}{2}$p?
4. Father bought two ties at 45p each, a pair of gloves at 98p and three pairs of socks at 35p per pair. What was his change from a five-pound note?
5. A refrigerator was reduced in price from 52 pounds to £44·80. By how much was it reduced?
6. A spin drier was reduced in price from £39·50 to £35·99. How much was saved by buying it at the sale?

At one shop all goods are to be reduced in price by 10p in each pound. Find what would be the sale prices of the following:

7. A washing machine at £45.
8. A three-piece suite at £97.
9. A dining suite at £85·50.

At a man's shop all goods are to be reduced in price by $12\frac{1}{2}$p in each pound. Find what can be saved by buying during the sale:

10. A suit costing £18·50 and a hat costing £2·25.
11. An overcoat costing £15·25, gloves costing £1·50 and two suits of pyjamas at £1·75 each.
12. A pair of shoes at £3·62$\frac{1}{2}$, three pairs of socks at $37\frac{1}{2}$p per pair and two shirts at £2·12$\frac{1}{2}$ each.

At a bargain counter all prices had been reduced by 20p in each pound. What would be the original price of:

13. A scarf which was marked at 80p?
14. A tie marked at 20p?
15. A waistcoat marked at £2·40?

1. Against each of the following put either "km" or "m" to show if you think they will be measured in kilometres or metres:
   length of a cricket pitch — distance travelled by car
   distance to the moon — length of a High Street

2. Draw a rectangle 7·6 cm by 5·8 cm and find the length of its diagonals.

3. How much should be left from a 50 m roll of braid after 25 drill bands, each 120 cm long, have been cut from it?

4. State the approximate breadth and length of a hall in metres if it is 22 paces wide and 35 paces long, my pace being 75 cm.

5. How far can I expect to travel between 9.30 a.m. and 1 p.m. at an average speed of 35 km per hour?

6. The drive to a garage is 15 m long and 3 m wide. How many paving slabs, each 100 cm by 75 cm, will be needed to cover the drive?

7. How many metres of material will be needed to make twenty desk covers, each 85 cm long?

8. How many tapes, each 25 cm long, can be cut from a roll containing 7·5 m of tape?

9. Mother needs four new curtains, each 210 cm long. If she allows 12 cm for a hem at the bottom and 8 cm for one at the top what is the total length, in metres, of the material required?

10. 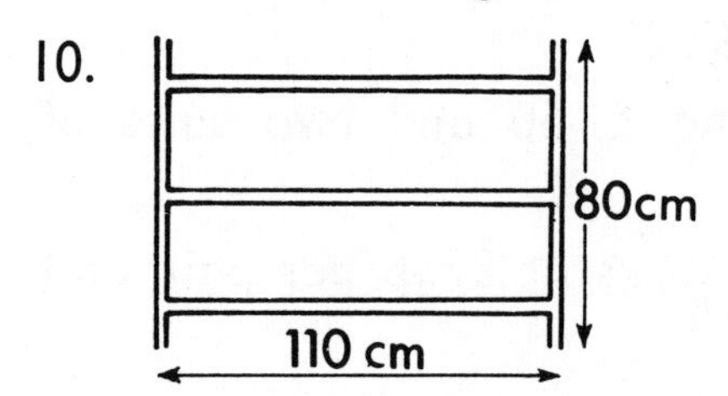

Father is going to make bookshelves for Toni's bedroom at the measurements shown in the sketch. He already has four lengths of suitable wood, each 115·5 cm long. Will Father have enough wood to make the shelves? If not, how much will he have to buy?

11. A stair of twelve steps leads from a ground floor to a landing, which is 105 cm wide. If each step is 18 cm high and 23 cm deep, what length of carpet will be needed to reach from the ground floor to the farther edge of the landing, allowing 20 cm extra for tucking in? A sketch will help.

1. A tare weight of a lorry is 2·36 metric tons. What should be the total weight when loaded with seventy-two 50 kg sacks of coal? Allow 2·5 kg for the weight of each sack.
2. The gross weight of a lorry loaded with sixty-five 50 kg sacks of coal is 5·19 metric tons. What is the tare weight of the lorry? Allow 3·2 kg for the weight of each wet sack.
3. What must be added to 863 kg to make 2·5 metric tons?
4. What must be taken from 3·25 metric tons to leave 2 750 kg?
5. What is the total weight of one thousand punnets of strawberries if the gross weight of each punnet is 250 grammes?
6. Complete this table:

Coins	Weight of		
	10	1	£1 worth
halfpennies	17·8 g		
pennies		3·56 g	
twos			356 g
			£5 worth
fives		5·65 g	
tens	113 g		
fifties	135 g		

7. At birth a baby weighed 2·86 kg. Exactly six months later its weight was 4·54 kg. What was the average gain per month?
8. Obtain a large jug or bottle or bulb bowl. Weigh it. Put in one litre of water and weigh again. What is the weight of 1 litre of water?
9. How many 500 gramme packets of rice can a grocer weigh out from a sack containing 50 kilogrammes?
10. What is the total weight of sugar on a shelf if there are 218 packets, each weighing 500 grammes, and 306 packets weighing 1 kg each?
11. How many 100 gramme packets of tea can be made up from a case containing 25 kilogrammes?

Roman Numerals

The numbers we use in arithmetic are called Arabic numerals. They are the digits 1, 2, 3, 4, 5, 6, 7, 8 and 9 together with the place-holder 0.
The Romans used letters instead of figures. They did not have place values to the base of ten as we do, but added or subtracted.
You will have used books which have the chapters numbered in Roman numerals, you will have seen clocks and watches having the hours marked with them, and some of the illustrations in your history books show dates in the same way. Here are some of them:

I	II	III	IV	V	VI	VII	VIII	IX	X	XI	XII	XIII	XIV
1	2	3	4	5	6	7	8	9	10	11	12	13	14

For these we have used only three letters: I, V and X. The others have been formed by adding or subtracting. Any letter can be used up to three times grouped together in one number, so we find that 3=I+I+I, but for 4 we have IV which means "one from five". In the same way we have 8=V+I+I+I and 9=I from 10.

In Roman numerals when a letter is followed by another of smaller value they are added to give the Arabic number (XXII=10+10+I+I).
Give the Arabic numbers equal to:

1. II   VII   XII   XV   XVIII   XX
2. XXI   XXVI   XXX   XXXV   XXXVI   XXVII   XXXII

In Roman numerals when a letter is followed by another of larger value the smaller is taken from the larger to give the Arabic number: XXIX= 10+10+(I from 10).

Give the Arabic numbers equal to:

3. IV   IX   XIV   XIX   XXIV   XXXIV   XXIX   XXXIX

Give the Roman numerals for:

4. 3   5   8   10   11   13
5. 16   22   4   9   34   29   17   25   19
6. 24   37   14   39   36

More Roman Numerals

So far we have added or subtracted with the letters I, V and X. The "only three times rule" has stopped us at 39. Other letters are needed. They are:

L=50 C=100 D=500 M=1 000

These letters bring in another rule. Since VV=X, LL=C and DD=M we can only use V, L and D one at a time.

Our rules now are:

(a) Letters I, X, C and M can be used in groups up to three at a time, e.g. MM=2 000, CCC=300.

(b) Letters V, L and D can be used only singly, e.g. XXV=25, CCL=250 and DLV=555.

(c) We add the values of letters except when one letter is followed by one of larger value and then we subtract. If other letters follow we continue to add, e.g.

XIV=10+(1 from 5) XCV=(10 from 100)+5
CDXIX=(100 from 500)+10+(1 from 10)
MMCMXCIX=1 000+1 000+(1 000−100)+(100−10)+(10−1)

DL=550 and CDXL=440. Give the Arabic numerals for:

1.	DCX	XLIV	CXLIX	DCCCII
2.	DCCV	DXCIX	CDXXXIV	DLXXVII

MDLX=1 560 and MML=2 050. Give the Arabic numerals for:

3.	MMV	MMMDL	MCDXLIX	MCCVI
4.	MCML	MMCMXL	DCCCLXXX	CMLXX
5.	XXVII	CCLXXV	CDLXXVI	CCXLV
6.	CLXIV	DCXLIV	CCXLVIII	CDXLIX
7.	MMMX	MCMLXI	MCDXLIV	CMXLVI

Give the Roman numerals for:

8.	3 006	2 040	2 500	980
9.	1 401	2 085	947	3 014
10.	1 599	3 900	486	1 505

Furnishing a Home

Price List			
Dining table	£24·80	Settee	£39·37½
Sideboard	£27·75	Easy chair	£18·62½
Dining chair	£6·75	Coffee table	£8·84
Carver chair	£7·45	Bookcase	£23·49
Corner cabinet	£13·90	Carpet	£46·70

1. Find the cost of two carver chairs.
2. Find the cost of a dining suite consisting of a sideboard, a dining table and 4 dining chairs.
3. Find the cost of a three-piece suite consisting of a settee and two easy chairs.
4. What will be the change from fifty pounds after paying for a sideboard and a corner cabinet?
5. What would be the new price of a dining chair if the present price was increased by 10p in the pound?
6. During a sale all prices were reduced by 12½p for each complete pound spent. What would be the saving on a suite consisting of a sideboard, a table, four chairs and two carvers?
7. How long will it take to pay for a carpet if £5·70 is paid at the time of the purchase and the rest is paid at 50p per week?
8. A customer is allowed to pay £10 at the time of purchase of a settee and three easy chairs. The rest is to be paid in equal monthly payments spread over one year on the first day of each month. What will be the monthly payment?
9. A customer bought a dining table, four dining chairs and a corner cabinet. How much extra did he pay by paying £10 at the time of purchase and making 15 monthly payments of £3·90?
10. A customer was allowed to pay £25 at the time of purchase and the rest in 18 equal monthly payments, for a carpet, a settee and two easy chairs. (a) What was the monthly payment, and (b) what was still owing at the end of a year if payments had been made at the proper time?

In *Second Problems* we found that the triangle numbers up to 30 were

3, 6, 10, 15, 21, 28.

1. Such numbers form a series. What are the next two?

We also found that there were square numbers, and those up to 30 were

4, 9, 16, 25.

2. These also form a series. What are the next two?
3. What is the square of 10? of 11? of 12?
4. What is the square root of 9? of 25? of 49?
5. What is the area of a square having sides 6 cm long?
6. What would be the length of the sides of a square having an area of 36 square metres?
7. What size square would have an area of 100 sq. m?

We found that 6 was a rectangle number as well as a triangle number: that it could be arranged as 2 by 3 or 3 by 2.

8. What is the area of a rectangle 2 cm by 3 cm?
9. What would be the width of a rectangle 3 cm long and having an area of 6 sq. cm?
10. What other rectangle forms 12 as well as 6 by 2?
11. What is the area of a rectangle 8 cm long and 2 cm wide?
12. What other size rectangle has an area of 16 sq. cm?
13. What would be the side of a square having an area of 64 sq. m?
14. Give the sizes of two rectangles that have the same area as a 6-centimetre square.
15. Give the sizes of two rectangles that have the same area as one that is 8 cm by 5 cm.
16. 2×2 is 2 squared, written as 2^2, and 5×5 is 5 squared, written as 5^2. What are these equal to? 3^2, 4^2, 7^2, 9^2.
17. 2 is the square root of 4, written as $\sqrt{4}$, and 3 is the square root of 9, written as $\sqrt{9}$. State the value of these square roots:
    $\sqrt{16}$ $\sqrt{25}$ $\sqrt{36}$ $\sqrt{100}$ $\sqrt{144}$
18. What size square has the same area as a rectangle four centimetres wide and twenty-five centimetres long?

Profit and Loss

1. If John weighed 26 kg 820 g in January and 27 kg 270 g in June what had he gained in weight?
2. A farmer had 314 sheep on the moors. After a blizzard he could only find 289 live sheep. What was his loss?
3. Mary bought a brooch for $62\frac{1}{2}$p. When she tried it on her new coat at home she did not like it. Her sister gave her 50p for the brooch. What was Mary's loss?
4. A shop-keeper paid $52\frac{1}{2}$p per dozen for toy soldiers which he sold for 6p each. How much profit per dozen did the shop-keeper make?
5. In a shop-window was shown a girl's hand-knitted jumper at £3·$92\frac{1}{2}$. Also shown was wool at $11\frac{1}{2}$p per 25 g and a pattern guide at 6p. Find (a) what it would cost to buy 500 g of wool and a pattern, (b) what is saved by knitting the jumper oneself instead of buying it ready made.
6. A dealer bought a motor-car for £380. He spent £15·73 to improve it. Find (a) the total cost of the car to the dealer, (b) what was his profit when he sold it for £445.
7. A greengrocer bought a ton of potatoes for £21 and sold them at $3\frac{1}{2}$p per kg. Find (a) the cost per 50 kilogrammes, (b) the selling price per 50 kilogrammes, (c) the amount of profit or loss per 50 kilogrammes.
8. In a store were 200 bales of cotton at a cost price of £2·75 per bale. After some were damaged by a burst pipe 48 were sold at £3·50 per bale, 115 were sold at £3 per bale and the rest were unsaleable. Find (a) how many were unsaleable, (b) the total value of the bales before the damage, (c) the total sale price of those sold, (d) the amount of profit or loss.
9. A man paid £2 300 for a house. At what price must he sell it to make £150 profit?
10. A shop-keeper bought 400 lettuces at 4p each. At what price must he sell them to make £10 profit?
11. A florist bought 300 carnations for £12. At what price each must he sell them so that his profit will be a half of the cost price?

Proportion

1. If one box holds 4 tennis balls how many will 5 boxes hold?
2. If one box holds 6 peaches how many boxes will hold 30 peaches?
3. 1 litre of water weighs 1 kg. What should 200 ml weigh?
4. Marbles are 8 for 1p. What is the cost of 2 dozen marbles?
5. If a tank holds 600 litres when full, how many will it hold (a) when $\frac{1}{3}$ full? (b) when $\frac{2}{3}$ full?
6. What is $\frac{2}{5}$ of £22·50?
7. Find $\frac{3}{7}$ of 13 m 30 cm.
8. $\frac{1}{3}$ of a journey takes 2 hr 45 mins. How long should the whole of the journey take at the same speed?
9. 25 boards covered $\frac{1}{4}$ of a fence. How many boards will be needed to cover the rest of the fence?
10. What should be paid, to the nearest penny, for 25 kg of potatoes at 3 kg for 10p?
11. A combine harvester cuts an average of 6 hectares in 4 hours. How many hectares should it cut in 10 hours?
12. A motorist completed a journey in 4 hours at an average speed of 48 km/h. What must be his average speed to complete the return journey in 3 hours?
13. If a car can travel 90 km on 12 litres of petrol, how far should it travel on 20 litres?
14. If potatoes are £25 per ton what should be charged for 400 kg?
15. If 15 m of wire netting cost £3·75 what should 25 m cost?

3 men dig 750 m^2 of garden in 2 days.

16. How much would they dig in 1 day?
17. How much would they dig in 5 days?
18. How long would it take 1 man to dig 750 m^2 of garden?
19. How long would it take 6 men to dig the same amount?
20. How much would 2 of these men dig in one day?

Posts and Rails

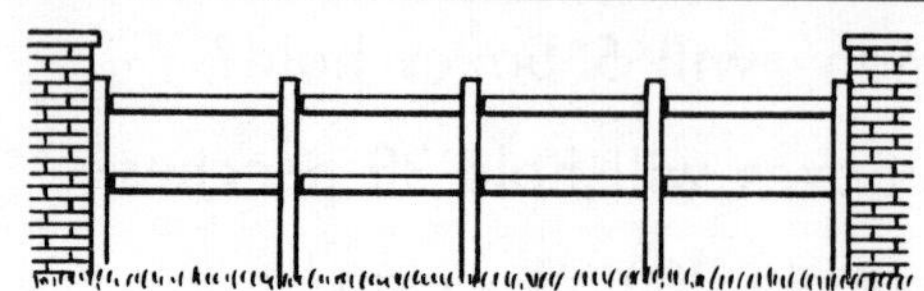

Each of these posts is 15 centimetres in thickness. The distance between any pair of posts is $1\frac{1}{2}$ metres.

1. How many posts are there? How many rails are there?
2. What is the total distance between the two brick walls?
3. If four posts had been used how many rails would there have been?
4. How many rails, placing two between each pair of posts, would be needed for a similar fence having (a) 12 posts? (b) 27 posts?

Here is a type of fence often seen in parks.

5. How many posts are there?
6. How many rails are there?
7. If there were to be three posts instead of two on each side of the square, how many posts would there be?
8. How many posts would be needed to put a fence completely round a rectangular plot, 55 m long and 20 m wide, placing one post at each $2\frac{1}{2}$ metres mark?
9. How many posts would be needed to put up a straight fence 26 m long, placing a post at each 200 cm?

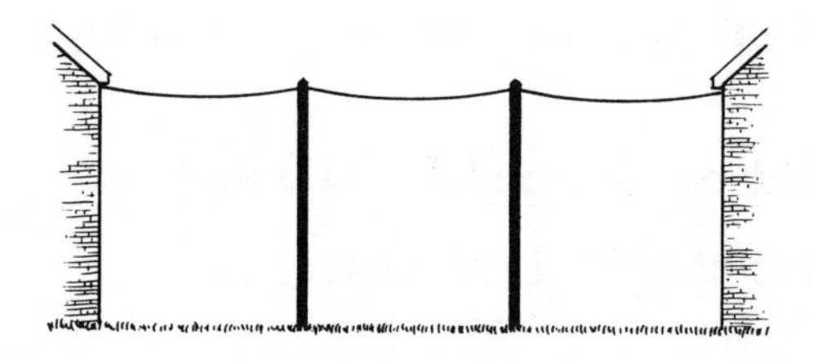

An electric cable is to be connected between two buildings that are 72 m apart. Its weight is to be supported by posts, evenly spaced between the two buildings.

10. At what distances should the posts be set if 3 are used?
11. At what distances should the posts be set if 5 are used?

In a street the lamp posts are spaced at intervals of 25 metres.

12. What will be the distance from the 1st lamp to the 4th?
13. What will be the distance from the 3rd lamp to the 9th?

Write answers only:

1. If a man walks at an average speed of 4 km/h how long should it take him to walk 12 kilometres?
2. How far should a man walk at 4 km/h if he walks for $1\frac{1}{2}$ hr?
3. A plane maintains an average speed of 600 km/h. How far should it travel in 2 hr? $\frac{1}{2}$ hr? $1\frac{1}{2}$ hr?
4. A motor car's petrol consumption averages 15 litres per 100 km. How far should it travel on 50 l? 10 l? 35 l?
5. The petrol consumption of a bus averages 40·5 litres per 100 km. How many litres of petrol will be used for 24 km? 90 km?

Here is a scale drawing (6 mm=10 km) representing a route travelled by A and B from opposite directions. The positions shown are reached after each has travelled for a half-hour, both having left at the same time

A start ↑ ——— A ——————————— B ——— ↑ B start

6. What are their respective average speeds?
7. How far apart should they be after a half-hour?
8. How far apart should they be after two hours?

Work in your book:

9. During a motor-car race a driver hopes to maintain an average speed of 94 km/h in a car which averages 15 litres per 100 km. How much petrol is he likely to need during 7 hours' driving?
10. A passenger is told that from Cardiff to Edinburgh is 600 km, and that the train is likely to average 120 km/h. How many pages of a book is he likely to read if he averages 36 pages per hr?

A car with two drivers sets out from Aberdeen at 6 p.m. on Monday to travel at an average speed of 60 km/h to Truro, a distance of 1 120 km. At the same time another car leaves Truro to travel to Aberdeen at an average speed of 70 km/h

11. At what time should the first car reach Truro?
12. At what time should the second car reach Aberdeen?
13. How far apart should the cars be at midnight on Monday?

Imperial Length

1. How many yards equal one-fifth of one mile?
2. What is the total distance of a motor-cycle race held over 12 laps on a course which is 3 ml. 6 fur. in length?
3. Mother has to make 8 curtains, each requiring 8 ft 3 in. of cloth. How many yards of material will she order?
4. Find the perimeter of a square with sides of 17 ft 10 in.
5. How long will each piece be if a board, 16 ft 11 in. long, is cut into 7 equal pieces?
6. Slabs 2 ft 6 in. long and 2 ft wide are to be laid for 70 yards along a footpath 10 ft wide. How many slabs will be needed?
7. How many pieces of wood, each 1 ft 3 in. long, can be cut from a plank that is 16 ft 6 in. long?
8. What length of braid will be needed to make 25 drill bands, each requiring 4 ft 8 in. of braid?
9. How many drill bands, each 4 ft 4 in. long, can be cut from 75 yd. of braid?
10. What was the original length of a roll of braid if 16 ft 10 in. are left after cutting off 11 lengths at 4 ft 10 in. each?
11. How much cable should be left on a half-mile drum if nine lengths $85\frac{1}{2}$ yd. each are cut from it?
12. What is the approximate length of a playground, in yards, if a boy walks it in 109 paces, and his pace averages 22 inches?
13. Find the cost of $7\frac{1}{2}$ yd. of gold braid at $1\frac{1}{2}$p an inch.

Here is a packing case made from boards, all of which are the same width and 1 in. thick.

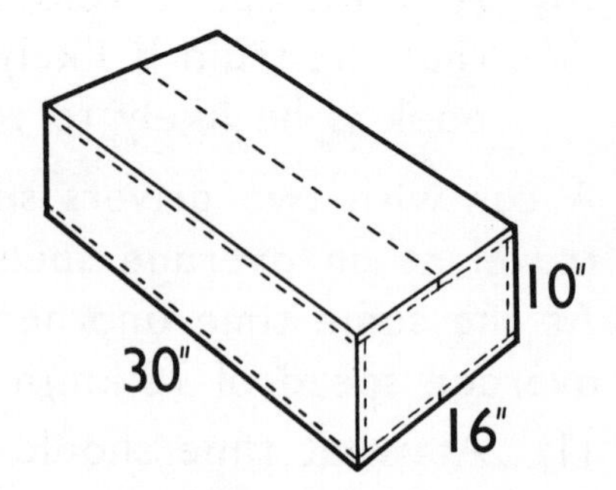

14. What is the width of the boards?
15. The boards will be of two different lengths. What are they?
16. What is the total length of board used to make one packing case?
17. What will be the cost of the timber to make 20 similar cases if that size timber costs 4p per foot?

1. When empty a lorry weighed 1 ton $17\frac{1}{2}$ cwt. and when loaded with coal 6 tons $5\frac{1}{2}$ cwt. How much coal was on the lorry?
2. What is the total weight of tea on a shelf if there are 342 quarter pound packets?
3. The average number of pupils for dinner is 136. The cook is allowed $\frac{3}{4}$ oz. of sugar per head for cooking purposes. What is the total amount of sugar used, to the nearest pound, in one school week?
4. Six similar railway trucks were found to contain 12 tons 8 cwt., 11 tons 18 cwt., 11 tons 16 cwt., 12 tons 9 cwt., 12 tons 10 cwt. and 11 tons 17 cwt. of coal respectively. What was the average contents of that type of truck?
5. A school's boilers used exactly 8 tons 16 cwt. of coke in exactly 11 days. What was the amount of coke used daily?
6. $2\frac{1}{2}$ cwt. of sugar is made up into one-pound packets. How many packets should there be?
7. What weight of white pepper will be needed to prepare one thousand one-ounce packets?
8. What weight will fill five hundred eight-ounce jars?

A grocer bought 5 cwt. of potatoes at £5·40 per hundredweight. He made them up into 25 bags each containing $\frac{1}{2}$ st. at 9p per bag, and the rest into 107 bags each containing $\frac{1}{4}$ st. at 5p per bag. The rest was dirt and unsaleable potatoes.

9. What was the total weight of the saleable goods?
10. What was the weight of the unsaleable portion?
11. What was the total selling price?
12. What was the profit or loss?

A merchant mixed 2 cwt. of tea at £420 per ton with 4 cwt. of tea at £380 per ton. The mixture was sold in quarter-pound packets at 8p per packet.

13. What was the cost of the mixture?
14. What was the increase of selling price over cost price?

Write answers only: (Note: details for No. 16 are on page 13.)

1. Through how many degrees does the minute hand of a clock move as it passes from the figure 2 to the figure 5?
2. Write in figures: twenty million nineteen thousand.
3. How far does a train travel in 20 minutes at 96 km/h?
4. What is the cost of 2 dozen pencils at $2\frac{1}{2}$p each?
5. Mary and Jane buy mother a present for 95p. If Mary pays 9p more than Jane how much does Mary pay?
6. How many twopenny cakes can be bought with four fives?
7. How many boxes will take 54 footballs if each box holds 8?
8. What is the perimeter of a seven-centimetre square?
9. What is the perimeter of a square having an area of twenty-five square metres?
10. How long must be a rectangle having an area of 120 square metres and a width of 8 metres?
11. What should I pay for $\frac{3}{4}$ m of silk at 90p per metre?
12. If eggs are 30p per dozen what should I pay for 5 eggs?
13. What should be the next number in this series? 1, 2, 4, 7, 11,.. ..
14. What should be the next number in this series? $\frac{1}{8}, \frac{1}{2}, \frac{7}{8}, 1\frac{1}{4}$,.. ..
15. How many 250 g jars can be filled from $7\frac{1}{2}$ kg of coffee?
16. How many litres will be needed to fill 5 dozen school milk bottles?
17. What change should there be from a £1 note after paying for $1\frac{3}{4}$ kg of beef steak at 52p per kilogramme?
18. If it takes Betty $\frac{1}{4}$ hr to walk to school, what is the latest time she should leave home to arrive at school by 8.50 a.m.?
19. What is the difference between 0·06 and 0·16?
20. What decimal quantity is equal to $2\frac{1}{4}$?
21. What is the difference between 1 m 8 cm and 1·8 cm?
22. What is the total value of 1 m 50 cm+1·24 m?
23. What is the value of 5 kg of potatoes at $\frac{1}{2}$ kg for 13p?
24. One-third of a class is outside sketching while the rest paint inside the class room. If there are 28 pupils in the room how many are outside?
25. The distance between two towns on a map is 2·8 cm. What is the actual distance if the map scale is 1 cm=5 km?

1. Find the average of the four consecutive numbers which follow 18.

2. A fair was open on weekdays from Monday, 23rd December 1968, to 3rd January 1969, inclusive. For how many days was it open?

3. Measure each of these lines to the nearest millimetre:

Here are some shop prices:
onions 7p per kg   beetroot 5p per kg   potatoes 9p per kg

4. Make out a bill for: $1\frac{1}{4}$ kg of beetroot, $2\frac{1}{2}$ kg of potatoes and 600 g of onions.

Here is a part of a time-table.

Capital	dep.	07.25	10.10	13.30
Village		10.26	13.08	16.25
Town		10.55	13.37	16.53
City	arr.	11.15	13.58	17.14

City	dep.	10.05	15.10	17.30
Town		10.27	15.33	17.53
Village		10.25	16.00	18.21
Capital	arr.	13.49	18.55	21.25

5. Which is the fastest train from Capital to City?

6. Which is the slowest train from City to Capital?

7. A man travels on the 07.25 train from Capital to City, and returns by the 17.30 train. How long is he in City?

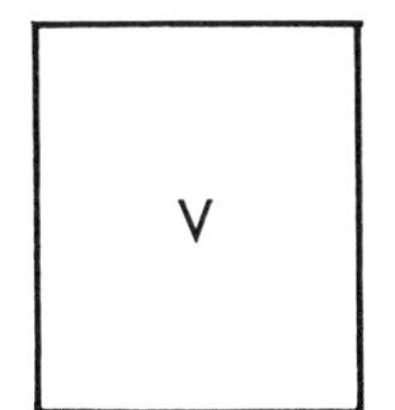

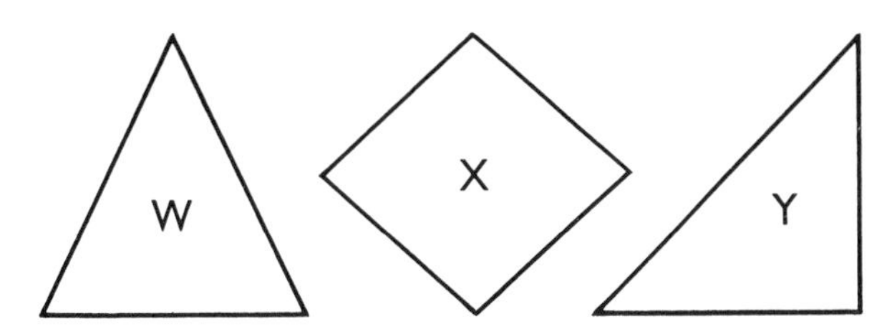

Z

8. Complete: (a) Figure. .   . .is a square.
(b) These figures have horizontal lines . .
(c) These figures have no vertical lines . .
(d) These figures are rectangles . .
(e) These figures have right angles . .
(f) These figures are triangles . .
(g) These figures are quadrilaterals . .

9. An estate agent bought a pair of houses for £4 350. He sold one for £1 955 and the other for £2 650. What was his gain?

10. A florist bought 5 000 crocus bulbs for £32. He sold 2 400 of them at 15p per doz.; 1 800 more at $12\frac{1}{2}$p per doz., and the rest at 20 for 11p. What was his profit?

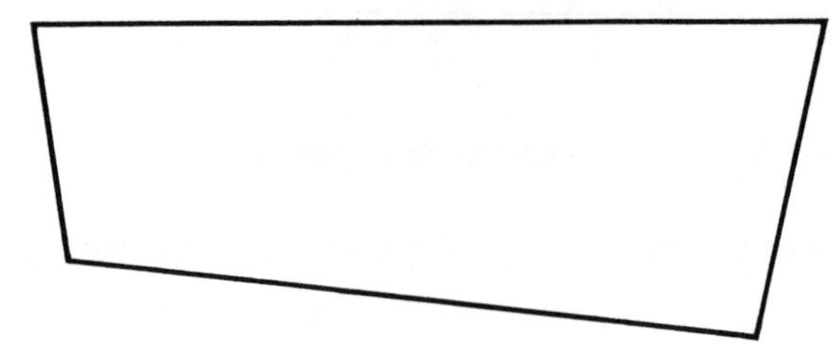

11. Find the perimeter of the field represented by this sketch.

Scale: 2 cm = 100 m

12. Find the cost of turfing a lawn 17 m by 36 m at 15p per sq. m.

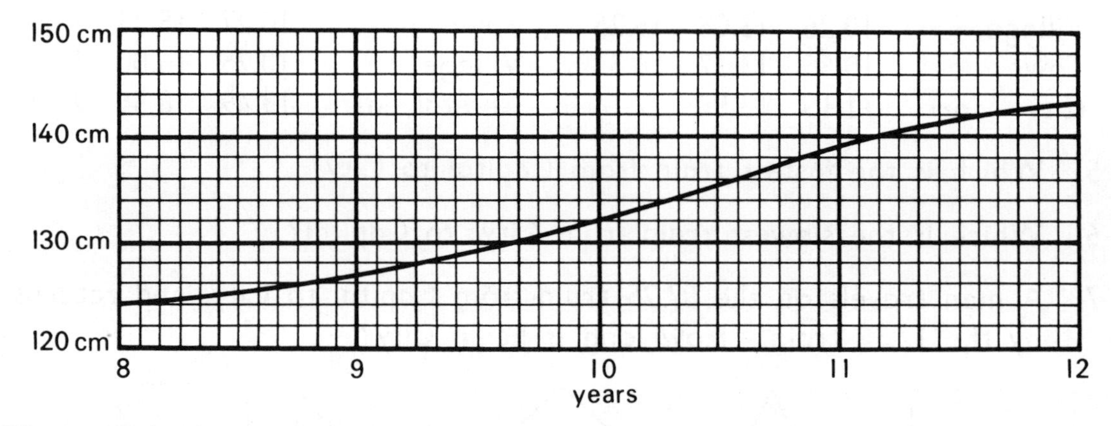

This graph shows the average heights of girls.

13. What is the average height of a girl $9\frac{1}{2}$ yr. old?

14. Sarah is 10 yr. 9 mth old. Her height is 141 cm. Is she of average height. If not, by how much does she differ?

15. 112 metres of wall are to be replaced by a fence. Posts are to be set at intervals of $1\frac{3}{4}$ metres. How many posts will be needed?

16. What should 750 kg of coal cost at £14 per ton?

17. During a test a car travelled 82 km on 15 litres of petrol. How many litres will be needed for a journey of 287 km?

Write answers only:

1. Find the length of a cruise, in 1970, which commences on 25th February and ends on 9th March, both dates inclusive.
2. Find the cost of a telephone call which costs $1\frac{1}{2}$p each 15 seconds and lasts for 5 minutes.
3. How many concert tickets at 15p each cost £1·20?
4. What should a dozen and a half stamps at $1\frac{1}{2}$p each cost?
5. What should a man earn at 33p per hour, working from 8 a.m. till 5.30 p.m., having one hour for lunch?
6. What part of five tons are 500 kilogrammes?
7. What is one-tenth of a half-million?
8. What is the next item in this series: 3, 5, 8, 12, 17?
9. How long will it take to save £2·50 at $12\frac{1}{2}$p per week?
10. Through how many degrees does the minute hand of a clock pass as it moves from the figure 3 to the figure 6?
11. What is the perimeter of a parallelogram having sides of 6 m and $2\frac{1}{2}$ m?
12. What size square would have a perimeter of one metre?
13. How much will each receive if Ann and Ada share 75p so that Ada has 12p more than Ann?
14. Which three consecutive numbers average 11?
15. What should be charged for 16 eggs at $22\frac{1}{2}$p per dozen?
16. How many 50 gramme packets can be made from $2\frac{1}{2}$ kg?
17. Which Roman numeral is half-way between XII and XVI?
18. What weight is one tenth of 2·5 tons?
19. What time in minutes is represented by 0·34 hr plus 0·26 hr?
20. If one metre=39·37 inches what does 1 cm equal in inches?
21. If lamp-posts are spaced at $18\frac{1}{2}$ m intervals how far is it from the 5th lamp to the 10th lamp?

Test 2

1. How much cheaper is it to buy one ton of coal at £18·25 than to buy it in small quantities at £1·95 per 100 kg?
2. A merchant mixes 1 kg of tea at 33p per kg, 2 kg at 30p per kg and 3 kg at 27p per kg. (a) What is the mixture worth per kg? (b) What price will make a profit of $9\frac{1}{2}$p per kg?
3. The time taken to cook a ham is found by allowing 20 minutes for each $\frac{1}{2}$ kg and adding another 20 min. Mother begins to cook $5\frac{1}{4}$ kg of ham at 10 a.m. At what time will it be cooked?
4. Find the perimeter of a rectangle $3\frac{1}{5}$ m wide and $5\frac{1}{4}$ m long.
5. A pole 6 metres long has to be cut into 2 parts, so that one is 44 cm longer than the other. How long is the shorter piece?
6. This line is drawn to a scale of 8 mm=5 km. What actual length does it represent? ——————————————
7. If it takes John 8 weeks to save £1·50 how long should it take him to save £3·75?
8. What should be the cost of a rectangular sheet of glass 180 cm by 150 cm at £1·60 per square metre?
9. Find the average temperature from these readings taken at hourly intervals: 60°, 63°, 63°, 64°, 62°, 61°, 61°.
10. If a car averages 11·67 litres per 100 km what will be the approximate cost for petrol at $6\frac{1}{2}$p per litre on a journey of 325 km?
11. During the sales 10p was allowed off each pound spent. What was saved on a fleecy-lined jacket at £10·10?
12. By how much has a piece of metal, 23·5 mm thick, to be reduced to make it 18·8 mm thick?
13. Find the perimeter of a triangle having sides of 8 cm 6 mm, 6 cm 4 mm and 4 cm 8 mm.
14. A man with a bulldozer removed 20 m of a hedge in $2\frac{1}{2}$ hours. How long should it take to remove $\frac{1}{4}$ km of similar hedge?
15. A street has 17 lamps spaced 45 m apart. If there is a lamp at each end, how long is the street?